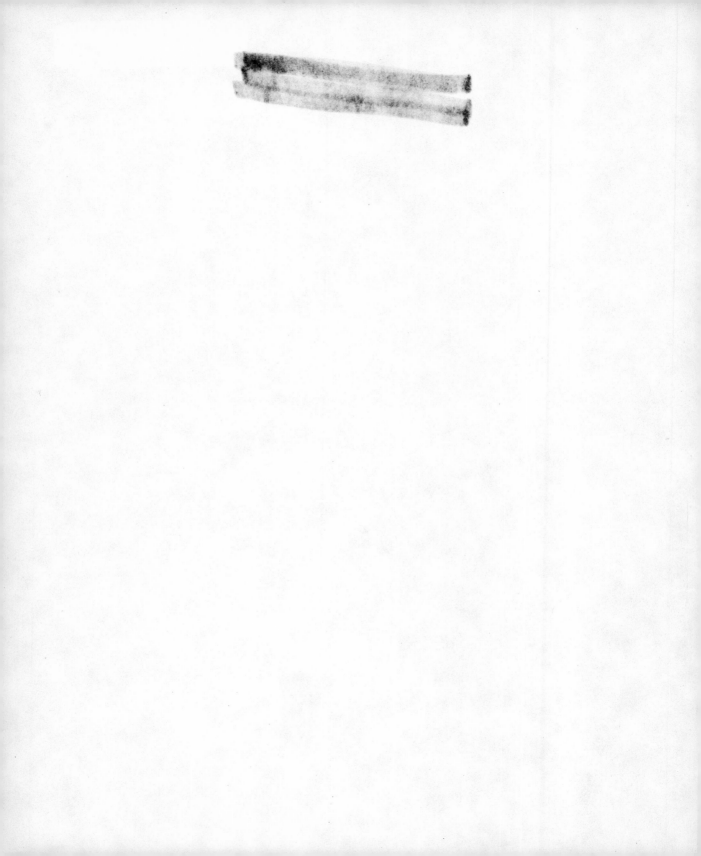

AMERICA the BEAUTIFUL

NORTH DAKOTA

By Margaret S. Herguth

Consultants

Theodore B. Jelliff, Red River High School, Grand Forks; author of *North Dakota, A Living Legacy*

Warren A. Henke, Ph.D., North Dakota historian; former professor of American History and North Dakota History, Bismarck State College

Curt Eriksmoen, Social Studies Coordinator, Department of Public Instruction, State of North Dakota

Robert L. Hillerich, Ph.D., Bowling Green State University, Bowling Green, Ohio

CHILDRENS PRESS®

CHICAGO

This shelter along the Little Missouri River was built in the 1930s by the Civilian Conservation Corps.

Project Editor: Joan Downing
Associate Editor: Shari Joffe
Design Director: Margrit Fiddle
Typesetting: Graphic Connections, Inc.
Engraving: Liberty Photoengraving

Library of Congress Cataloging-in-Publication Data

Herguth, Margaret S.
   America the beautiful. North Dakota / by Margaret S.
Herguth.
      p.   cm.
   Includes index.
   Summary: Introduces the geography, history,
government, economy, industry, culture, historic
sites, and famous people of the Flickertail State.
   ISBN 0-516-00480-8
   1.   North Dakota—Juvenile literature.
[1.   North Dakota.]   I.   Title.
F636.3.H47   1990   89-25283
978.4—dc20   CIP
                                         AC

Food being served at the 1989 Centennial celebration

TABLE OF CONTENTS

Chapter 1

THE SPIRIT OF NORTH DAKOTA

THE SPIRIT OF NORTH DAKOTA

Scratch the soil and the finest crops spring up.
Thrust a shrub in the earth and it bears fruit.
—North Dakota's commissioner of agriculture
and labor, in 1908

Another North Dakotan later had a less cheerful view than the commissioner of agriculture quoted above. Writer-broadcaster Eric Sevareid, who grew up in Velva, said it was "a trial of the human spirit just to live there, and a triumph of faith and fortitude for those who stayed on through the terrible blasting of the summer winds, the merciless suns, through the frozen darkness of the winters. . . . "

Both visions are accurate. Barely one hundred years old, this Great Plains state has always been a land of struggle and contrast.

North Dakota has been labeled a "passage state," a state that people pass through to get someplace else. For several years, civic leaders have struggled to change this label. Their work is paying off. In 1988, tourism added more than $600 million to the state income. During the late 1980s, record numbers of North Dakotans and out-of-state vacationers camped in the parks, saw the historic sites, and shared in the many festivals.

Today's North Dakotans still struggle, mostly against a troubled farm economy. But they are heading toward the twenty-first century with the spirit of determination shown by their predecessors, working to control their own destiny.

Chapter 2

THE LAND

THE LAND

SETTING THE STAGE

Hundreds of millions of years ago, geologists say, land and sea fought to dominate the area that is North Dakota. The land sank and the salt sea rose over it. Then the land reappeared. This happened several times, the last about 70 million years ago when the sea receded permanently.

For millions of years, more changes took place below the surface of the land and beneath the sea than took place above. North Dakota's valuable resources were forming. Sediment left by the sea became limestone, sandstone, and shale deposits. These deposits, along with the remains of early plant and sea life, were the beginnings of large oil and lignite coal supplies.

Then, about a million years ago, the North American climate cooled. It didn't happen suddenly, like a modern-day North Dakota blizzard, but season after season, as more snow fell than the sun could melt. The hardened snow ultimately formed glaciers.

The powerful ice sheets erased much of the old North Dakota landscape and created a new one. Bulldozing their way across the land, the glaciers leveled existing hills and built others. They etched out shallow potholes and formed deep lakes. There is evidence that at least two—and perhaps up to ten—glaciers formed, melted, and re-formed over thousands of years. The glaciers that sculpted most of North Dakota's present landscape disappeared some thirteen or fourteen thousand years ago.

GEOGRAPHY

Nature's changes above and below the ground dwarf the changes made by men and women. People, however, drew boundaries around the land that nature shaped.

Spread comfortably over 70,702 square miles (183,118 square kilometers), North Dakota ranks seventeenth in size of all the fifty states. It has the distinction of lying exactly in the middle of the North American continent. A stone monument, or cairn, near Rugby marks the midpoint. From there it is about 1,500 miles (2,414 kilometers) to the continental boundaries at the Arctic Ocean, the Gulf of Mexico, the Atlantic Ocean, and the Pacific Ocean.

Only the meandering Red River of the North and the Bois de Sioux River on the eastern border break the precision of North Dakota's rectangular outline. From top to bottom, between Canada and South Dakota, North Dakota measures 210 miles (338 kilometers). The expanse between Minnesota and Montana varies. In the slightly narrower north, it is 310 miles (499 kilometers) across the state. At the broader base, the distance from east to west is 360 miles (579 kilometers).

TOPOGRAPHY

If escarpments and topography determined state boundaries, North Dakota would be three different states. Though most of the state shares a glacial heritage, there are three separate regions

The fertile Red River Valley has the best topsoil in the state.

marked by escarpments, or natural ridges, that define changing
elevations. The three regions also have different soils, grasses, and
rain levels. Because of these distinctions, the three sections of
North Dakota have somewhat different agricultural specialties.
Topography has also contributed to population changes and
overall economic development within the regions.

THE RED RIVER VALLEY

The easternmost region is the Red River Valley, which extends
into neighboring Minnesota. North Dakota's portion of the Red
River Valley is a flat, narrow, exceptionally fertile strip only about
30 to 40 miles (48 to 64 kilometers) wide, extending from Canada
to South Dakota. It is named for the Red River of the North,
which carved a winding channel from Wahpeton to Pembina.

Elevation above sea level in this region is the lowest in the state, declining from about 965 feet (294 meters) in the south to under 800 feet (244 meters) at Pembina.

Despite its name, the Red River Valley is not truly a valley but a lake bed. Thousands of years ago, it was the bottom of glacial Lake Agassiz, so-named in the nineteenth century for the Swiss glacial geologist Louis Agassiz. Formed when the glacial ice melted in eastern North Dakota and western Minnesota, Lake Agassiz covered more than 100,000 square miles (259,000 square kilometers) on both sides of the Red River of the North. Although it drained into Hudson Bay and disappeared long ago, several small lakes and remnants of the sand beaches still exist.

Thanks to glacial action, opportune winds, and tall grasses, the Red River Valley has the best topsoil in the state. Crops including wheat, potatoes, and sugar beets grown in the rich black earth are among the best in the world.

THE DRIFT PRAIRIE

Just west of the Red River Valley is the Drift Prairie, named for the glacial deposits of gravel, or drift. Marking the change between regions is the Pembina Escarpment, a ridge that extends from the Canadian border to the southern part of the state.

The Drift Prairie, more than 200 miles (322 kilometers) wide at the top of North Dakota, narrows to about 70 miles (113 kilometers) at the bottom. This gently rolling plain, used extensively for farming, is also North Dakota's lake country and a popular recreation area. The Drift Prairie is higher than the Red River Valley, rising gradually from 1,400 feet (427 meters) above sea level in the south to over 2,000 feet (610 meters) in the Turtle Mountains to the north. The Turtle Mountains, one of the few

The Turtle Mountain region is one of the few wooded areas in the state.

wooded areas in the state, cover some 800 square miles (2,072 square kilometers).

Early explorers discovered that the tallest grasses and richest soil on the prairie occurred east of the 100th meridian (100 degrees longitude). West of the 100th meridian, where rainfall was considerably less, they discovered shorter grasses and soils that were lighter in color. Some explorers dubbed the land west of this invisible but abrupt line the "Great American Desert."

The 100th meridian cuts through the Drift Prairie. Although much of this region has good soil and produces excellent crops, brown soil with a thinner surface layer and shorter grasses begins to appear in the western part.

THE MISSOURI PLATEAU

The third natural region in North Dakota is the Missouri Plateau. Startlingly different from the other two regions, the

Horses grazing on the short prairie grasses of the Missouri Plateau

Missouri Plateau is separated from the Drift Prairie by the
Missouri Escarpment. This ridge rises sharply some 400 feet (122
meters) above the Drift Prairie. Another belt of hills, between the
Missouri Escarpment and the Missouri River, marks the stopping
point of glacial movement in North Dakota. It is known as the
Coteau du Missouri—the hills of Missouri. This stony ridge was
formed from the debris dropped along the edge of the last melting
glacier. Some of the hills are separated by meadows and prairies.
Many are not much more than piles of stone.

The Missouri Plateau reaches a remarkable elevation for being
part of a low-lying plains state. It varies from about 1,800 feet (549
meters) above sea level near the Missouri River to 3,184 feet (970
meters) at Rhame, in the southwest corner. Although Rhame is
the highest town in the state, White Butte—a few miles to the
northeast—is the highest geographical point. Measured at 3,506
feet (1,069 meters) above sea level, White Butte is one of the
hundreds of flat-topped, slope-sided, steeply rising remnants of

water erosion across the plateau. Geologists who have studied the ancient layers of lignite and other minerals in the sides of these distinctive hills found that they line up, or match, from butte to butte. This is part of the proof that the area was once an unbroken piece of land. Some thin glacial deposits are found on the Missouri Plateau, but the southwest area, or Missouri Slope, is entirely unglaciated. Water and wind erosion rather than glaciers created the hills, valleys, gorges, and ravines.

Some farmers raise crops on the Missouri Plateau. But these western lands—with their rocks, hills, and short grasses—are better for grazing. This region is North Dakota's cattle country.

THE BADLANDS

North Dakota's greatest scenic treasure and most important wildlife preserve is the Badlands in the Slope section of the Missouri Plateau. The Sioux Indians called it *Mako Shika*, or "land bad." Early white travelers through the maze of buttes, rocks, valleys, and ravines labeled the land along the Little Missouri River as "grand, dismal, and majestic." In the 1860s, United States Army General Alfred Sully is reported to have called the Badlands "hell with the fires put out." Actually, the fires still burn. Outcroppings of lignite in the buttes are ignited by lightning and burn for years. The red scoria (refuse from the lignite fires) adds to the palette of greens, golds, blues, silvers, browns, and blacks in the landscape.

The Badland's most notable supporter, Theodore Roosevelt, first came in 1883 to hunt buffalo and returned later to be a rancher. Teddy Roosevelt never lost his love and fascination for the rugged and mysterious land. The 70,374-acre (28,480-hectare) Theodore Roosevelt National Memorial Park is named for this American

Among the sights to be seen in the rugged Badlands of Theodore Roosevelt National Memorial Park are hills that have been eroded by wind and water (left), red scoria left on the hills by lignite fires (bottom left), and petrified forests (bottom right).

The Little Missouri River, as seen from Wind Canyon Trail

conservationist who was also the twenty-sixth president of the United States.

The North Dakota Badlands are good lands today, for traveler and rancher alike. Modern roads plus trails for hikers and horseback riders allow easy access through much of the maze. The grassy valleys with their protective hills feed and shelter cattle year-round.

RIVERS, LAKES, AND RESERVOIRS

Nearly 1,500 square miles (3,885 square kilometers) of the vast farming state of North Dakota is covered by water — inkblot-shaped lakes, winding rivers, huge reservoirs, glacial potholes, and ponds.

The Missouri River and its tributaries, including the Yellowstone, Little Missouri (which carved out the Badlands), Knife, Heart, and Cannonball, drain between half and two-thirds of the state. At one time, the Missouri River flowed north. Later, it was turned south by the glaciers. It carries North Dakota's western runoff water into the Mississippi and ultimately into the Gulf of Mexico. Another important tributary of the Missouri is the James River. The two rivers are separated by many miles in North Dakota, however, joining at the southern border of South Dakota.

Eastern North Dakota waters drain north into Hudson Bay via the Red River of the North and the Mouse River. The Mouse River is actually a tributary of the Red River, but joins the Red in Canada. Known as the Souris River in Canada, the Mouse flows down from Saskatchewan into north-central North Dakota, turns east, and flows back up into Manitoba. Other major tributaries of the Red River are the Sheyenne, Pembina, Park, and Goose rivers.

Because river levels rise and fall dramatically depending on the amount of rain and sudden snow melt-off, hundreds of dams have been built. Several big dams provide not only flood control and municipal water supplies but irrigation, navigation, and electric power as well. Reservoirs of the dammed water are also used for recreation and wildlife refuges.

North Dakota's premier dam is Garrison, completed in 1954 to harness the state's most important river, the flood-prone Missouri. Located 75 miles (121 kilometers) up the Missouri River from Bismarck, Garrison Dam is one of the largest rolled-earth dams in the world. Its reservoir, Lake Sakakawea, is a water-lover's paradise. With a surface of 368,000 acres (148,926 hectares) and snaking 178 miles (286 kilometers) west and north from the dam, Lake Sakakawea is the largest man-made lake entirely within a single state.

A few lakes in North Dakota serve as internal drainage systems where the rivers don't offer outlets for the runoff. Devils Lake and Stump Lake, inland glacial lakes with no outlets, are part of an internal drainage complex. The Powers Lake complex and Long Lake are two other drainage systems.

Although Devils Lake is the largest natural lake in the state, its water level has receded and it is salty. If proposed plans are carried out through the Garrison Diversion Project, an opening will be made in landlocked Devils Lake, flow will increase, and the brackishness will disappear.

CLIMATE AND WEATHER

North Dakota, in the center of the North American continent, has what is called a continental climate. This means there are four distinct seasons, rapid temperature changes, limited rainfall, and low humidity. Winters tend to be long and cold, summers relatively short and hot.

The average January temperature is 3 degrees Fahrenheit (minus 16 degrees Celsius) in the northeast part of the state and 14 degrees Fahrenheit (minus 10 degrees Celsius) in the southwest. In July, the temperature averages 67 degrees Fahrenheit (19 degrees Celsius) in the north and 73 degrees Fahrenheit (23 degrees Celsius) in the south.

Temperature fluctuations recorded in North Dakota have been among the greatest of the entire North American continent. Two records set in 1936 still stand. A frigid minus 60 degrees Fahrenheit (minus 51 degrees Celsius) was recorded at Parshall, near Lake Sakakawea, in February 1936. In July of that year, Steele, east of Bismarck, reached a scorching 121 degrees Fahrenheit (49 degrees Celsius).

When North Dakota weather "follows the rules" by bringing enough but not too much sunshine and precipitation, farmers grow record crops and ranchers produce outstanding livestock. But this land of weather extremes keeps farmers and ranchers on their toes.

The statistics sound reasonable enough. The sun shines 65 percent of the time in the summer and an average of 2,680 hours year-round. Although rainfall averages only about 14 inches (36 centimeters) annually in the west and about 22 inches (56 centimeters) in the east, more than 75 percent of it comes at the most important time for crops: May, June, and July.

But there are dozens of weather surprises for every "average" weather statistic. A warm westerly Chinook wind can boost winter temperatures in a twenty-four-hour period. Sudden spring thaws after heavy winter snows create flood conditions, even with the state's many dams. In 1979, the Red River at Grand Forks rose almost 50 feet (15 meters), more than 20 feet (6 meters) above flood level. It was the state's worst flood of the twentieth century.

Strong winds, with few trees and no mountain ranges to slow them down, bring both blizzards and dust storms. Modern weather forecasting prevents most loss of life in snowstorms today. But North Dakota weather history contains stories of whole buildings, livestock, and travelers buried beneath drifts.

In the 1930s, when drought, dust, and depression dominated the land, North Dakota's dry topsoil blew all the way to the East Coast and out to the Atlantic Ocean. The spring and summer drought of 1988, though not as devastating, has been compared to that of the 1930s.

The weather and the increased isolation it caused defeated many North Dakotans, but it strengthened others. Then and now, they bet their lives on the weather and on the crops.

Chapter 3
THE PEOPLE

THE PEOPLE

*I think topography affects character,
and there is no place for devious behavior
in the wide open spaces.*
—North Dakota Horizons Magazine

It must be true that there is no place for devious behavior in the wide open spaces. In the late 1980s, North Dakota had a prison population of just over four hundred. North Dakota has by far the lowest violent crime rate of any state, and the second-lowest property crime rate.

A statistic North Dakotans would like to reverse, however, is the rate at which residents move away. Invariably loyal to their home state, hundreds of thousands of North Dakota natives nonetheless have moved to other states.

POPULATION

In the 1980s, there were an estimated one million people still living who had been born in North Dakota. Only about 400,000 of them still lived in the state. Over the years, 600,000 had moved away. Some moved to escape the isolation and rugged weather. Most, however, sought new or better-paying jobs.

The Great Depression of the 1930s spurred the largest emigration from the state. Farm failures and too few nonagricultural jobs forced many North Dakotans to seek jobs in other states. From 1930, when there was an official all-time high population of 680,845, the census figure has bounced like a yo-yo.

23

Population dropped through the 1930s and 1940s, bounced back up in the 1950s, then dropped again in the 1960s.

Finally, in the 1970s, the figures took another upward swing. By 1980, there were 652,717 people living in the fifty-three counties of North Dakota.

The yo-yo is still in motion. The Census Data Center at North Dakota State University reported an estimated population of 684,917 in 1985, and a drop down to just over 679,000 in 1986. But if projections made by the center are on target, North Dakota could have nearly 800,000 people by the year 2000.

POPULATION DISTRIBUTION

For the first time in its history, urban dwellers number just over half of the state's population. The number of North Dakotans living in rural areas—open country or towns with fewer than 2,500 people—dropped from almost 410,000 in 1960 to about 337,000 in 1986.

There is still a lot of unpopulated land in the state, however. Population density in North Dakota is only 9.2 people per square mile (3.5 people per square kilometer). And thirty-six of the state's fifty-three counties were still listed in 1986 as 100 percent rural, having no towns of 2,500 people.

In 1986, only twenty-one North Dakota towns could be called urban centers—cities with 2,500 people or more. The four top cities—Fargo, Bismarck, Grand Forks, and Minot—had a combined population of about 200,000.

Early towns were founded to serve the farmers, but only those towns on a railroad line or a navigable river prospered past the early boom days. When the Northern Pacific Railroad was about to cross the Red River from Moorhead, Minnesota, in the winter

A Norwegian display at the North Dakota Heritage Center recalls the ancestry of many North Dakotans.

of 1871-72, a "tent city" of squatters and railroad workers sprang up on the site that would be Fargo. By 1890, Fargo had more than 5,000 people. One hundred years later, it is still the biggest city in North Dakota and the only one with more than 60,000 residents.

The rough port town of Edwinton, on the Missouri River, also prospered when the railroad came. Named originally for a Northern Pacific Railroad official, Edwinton was renamed Bismarck in honor of the chancellor of Germany. Bismarck was also the chosen city for some political maneuvering. Politicians with strong ties to the Northern Pacific voted to move the Dakota territorial capital to Bismarck from the geographically undesirable Yankton (South Dakota), in the southeast.

WHO ARE THE NORTH DAKOTANS?

About 98 percent of all North Dakotans were born in the United States. Most of them are descendants of the Norwegian, German, German-Russian, English, Irish, Scottish, Welsh,

About 48 percent of North Dakotans are members of the Lutheran church.

Swedish, and Danish immigrants who came to the area in the eighteenth and early nineteenth centuries.

Large groups of immigrants created ethnic colonies in different sections of North Dakota. Norwegians were the largest group to settle in North Dakota and lived primarily in the Red River Valley. German-Russians—descendants of the Germans who left their homeland and went to Russia in the eighteenth and early nineteenth centuries—came to many counties in central North Dakota. The Irish and English tended to settle in the western ranch lands.

In 1910, with the heaviest influx over, more than 70 percent of all North Dakota residents had been born in another country or had a foreign-born parent. About 125,000 of a total state population of 577,000 were Norwegian. Germans and German-Russians totaled about 117,000. There were 73,000 English, Irish, Scottish, and Welsh. And there were tens of thousands of Swedes and Danes. Small French, Polish, Finnish, Icelandic, Dutch, Belgian, Bulgarian, Greek, Armenian, and Russian settlements dotted the prairie.

Nearly twenty-two thousand Native Americans live throughout North Dakota. More than one-third live on the Turtle Mountain Indian Reservation at the top of the state, home of the Turtle

The Fort Totten Indian Reservation, south of Devils Lake, is the home of the Devils Lake Sioux.

Mountain Chippewas. Other reservations are Fort Berthold, at Lake Sakakawea, home of the Mandans, Hidatsas, and Arikaras; Fort Totten, south of Devils Lake, home of the Devils Lake Sioux; and Standing Rock, in the south, home of the Standing Rock Sioux. Although some Native Americans live in the North Dakota section of the Sisseton Reservation, in the far southeastern part of the state, they are counted among South Dakota's Indians.

There was an almost 50 percent increase in so-called minorities in North Dakota during the 1970s. Although they are counted in the hundreds, not the thousands, the Filipino population more than doubled and the Chinese population grew almost 85 percent. Hundreds of Koreans, Vietnamese, and Indians from India came to North Dakota. The black population, which numbered almost 2,600 in 1980, increased by 3 percent in the 1970s. The state's Native American and Eskimo population increased 40 percent during that decade and has stayed near the 20,000 mark.

Most North Dakotans are Protestants, and about 48 percent are members of the Lutheran church. About 38 percent are Roman Catholic, and most of the rest are Methodist, Presbyterian, or United Church of Christ. Nearly five thousand Mormons (members of the Church of Jesus Christ of Latter-day Saints) also live in North Dakota.

Chapter 4
THE BEGINNING

THE BEGINNING

*Well, America, you understand, in those days
was different. It was a nice place, but you
wouldn't believe it if you saw it today. Without
buses, without trains, without states,
without Presidents, nothing!*
—Stephen Vincent Benét, ''Jacob and the Indians''

ANCIENT NORTH DAKOTANS

It was not until the last glacier retreated that people began to occupy the plains. Several groups of human beings inhabited the North Dakota area beginning some ten to fifteen thousand years ago. No one knows exactly when they came, but the big-game hunters, nomads, and woodland people left clues.

The first group, the Paleo Indians, probably crossed from Asia to Alaska and migrated south to Dakota. They hunted the elephantlike mammoths and mastodons. Archaeologists believe they camped on the Missouri River near what is now New Town, North Dakota. A group of later nomads left behind remnants of their culture—knives, dart points, and stone tools.

The early people traveled back and forth across the plains, stopping where they found food and water. Droughts struck the plains thousands of years ago just as they do now. People probably left drought-stricken areas when vegetation dried up and animals died or left. When the climate changed and moisture returned, so did the animals and the people.

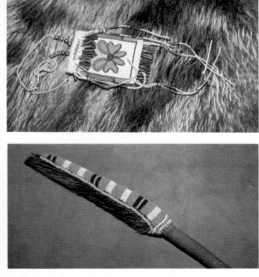

The Arikaras (left) and the Hidatsas (who made the strike-a-lite and the porcupine-quill hairbrush shown above) were among the tribes of Indians who lived in the state before the white explorers arrived.

NORTH DAKOTA'S NATIVE AMERICANS

Like white settlers who would come to North Dakota from many nations and states, American Indians belonged to different nations and tribes. Five major tribes lived in North Dakota: the Mandans, Hidatsas, Arikaras, Chippewas, and Sioux (or Dakotas). At least four other tribes traded in the area: the Assiniboines and Crees, who were close allies, the Cheyennes, and the Crows.

The Mandans, part of the Siouan language group, appear to have been the first modern tribe in the area. Archaeologists have discovered bones, dishes, and arrowheads that show the Mandans' route up the Missouri Valley from the southeast. More than 250 years ago, the first white explorer known to travel through North Dakota discovered their villages and earthen lodges near the city that bears their name.

The Mandans, Hidatsas, and Arikaras lived in villages along the Missouri River. They built permanent earth-lodge homes, hunted buffalo, and farmed.

A group of western North Dakota métis pose in 1883 with their distinctive Red River carts.

The Chippewas, who moved west from Minnesota, were forest Indians who settled in the Turtle and Pembina mountain areas of northeastern North Dakota. Many still live on the Turtle Mountain Indian Reservation near the Canadian border.

During the early fur-trading days, many French traders married Chippewa and Cree women. The children, and subsequent generations born of these unions, were called *métis*. Legally considered Indians, the métis had many French characteristics and were proud of both their Indian and French heritage. The métis spoke a mixture of French, Chippewa, and Cree.

The métis contributed to successful trading in the Red River Valley. They are credited with developing the Red River cart, one of the earliest vehicles used to carry goods on the prairie. Fitted with two high wheels and pulled by an ox, the wooden wagon could carry a 1,000-pound (454-kilogram) load on the uneven prairie sod.

The largest tribe of the Siouan language family and the one that most affected North Dakota was the Dakota, or Sioux. During the seventeenth century, the Sioux numbered about twenty-five thousand.

The Sioux, a name synonymous with Indian wars on the plains, were feared by both white settlers and other Indians. But apart from being warriors, the Sioux were a highly structured and democratic nation. They called themselves *Oceti Sakowin*, or Seven Council Fires, referring to their seven political divisions.

Four divisions—Mdewakanton, Sisseton, Wahpeton, and Wahpekute—made up the Eastern, or Santee, Sioux. Yankton and Yanktonai made up the Middle, or Yankton, Sioux. The largest division of all, the Teton, made up the Western Sioux.

The Teton Sioux, with about twelve thousand members, were masters of the plains. As they moved into what is now North Dakota, the Teton Sioux pushed other tribes from their lands. Skilled warriors, excellent horsemen, and taller than their fellow Sioux, the Teton terrorized white settlers who took their land. Numerous battles were fought between the United States Army and the Sioux.

THE FIRST EUROPEANS

The people who came to North Dakota in the 1700s and early 1800s were after adventure, business opportunities, and profit. But it was a slow beginning on the plains.

A fur trader and former soldier from Canada named Pierre Gaultier de Varennes, Sieur de La Vérendrye, was the first white person known to visit North Dakota. He had heard stories from Indians in Canada about a great river that flowed to the western sea and was determined to find this water route to the Pacific.

In 1731, the La Vérendrye party began an incredible journey across the uncharted territory of lower Canada. The trip was both

Two of North Dakota's early Indians were Four Bears, a Mandan painted by George Catlin (left), and Two Ravens, a Hidatsa painted by Karl Bodmer (right).

physically demanding and dangerous. The men built trading posts and supply depots along their route, staying in each new post for a time to trade with the Indians.

On October 18, 1738, La Vérendrye and his party of fifty-two men—Indians and whites—left Fort La Reine, which they had built in Canada above North Dakota. A large band of Assiniboine Indians joined La Vérendrye and his group on the way. The combined party that reached a Mandan village near present-day Menoken on December 3, 1738, has been estimated at more than a thousand. After less than two weeks with the Mandans, and in the dead of winter, La Vérendrye and his companions walked back to Fort La Reine, a journey that took almost two months.

Although La Vérendrye was unable to find a water route to the Pacific Ocean, his difficult journeys were valuable to all who followed. He was the first to write about his travels in North Dakota and about Indian life there.

DAVID THOMPSON

In 1797, the North West Company, one of the largest fur-trading businesses in North America, sent a new employee on a special mission. David Thompson, a precise, energetic surveyor-geographer from Canada, was given several tasks. He was to find the 49th parallel, which would become the official boundary between Canada and the United States. In addition, Thompson was to find all trading posts belonging to the North West Company and determine which were north or south of the 49th parallel. The company also wanted Thompson to visit the Mandan Indians on the Missouri River.

David Thompson traveled some 50,000 miles (80,465 kilometers) during his lifetime and accurately mapped the main travel routes through more than 1 million miles (1,609,300 kilometers) of Canadian and United States territory. He was the first to map part of what is now North Dakota. He is also credited with discovering Turtle Lake, one of the sources of the Mississippi River. Thompson's descriptions of Mandan and Hidatsa homes, manners, dress, and farming practices were considerably more detailed than La Vérendrye's earlier notes had been. A huge globelike monument honoring David Thompson for his contributions to North Dakota was erected near Minot.

ALEXANDER HENRY THE YOUNGER

Alexander Henry the Younger, nephew of a fur trapper also named Alexander Henry, was a Canadian fur trader who worked for the vast North West Company. He was described as shrewd, serious, and intensely interested in making money. In 1801, Henry the Younger established the first long-term trading post in North Dakota at Pembina, in the northeastern tip of North Dakota's Red River Valley. It was to become the nucleus for the first white settlement in the state. At least three earlier fur-trading posts had been built in North Dakota, but none lasted long.

Not only was Henry a successful trader-businessman for the North West Company, he was an excellent record keeper. His daily journals offer the best written record of the early intermingling of white traders and Indians in the Red River Valley between 1800 and 1808.

Henry was also the first white man known to have farmed in North Dakota. Tired of a diet of buffalo meat and other wild game, fish, and wild fruits, Henry planted his first garden in 1803. That year he harvested hundreds of bushels of potatoes, cabbages, carrots, onions, turnips, beets, and parsnips. Henry's garden prospered until 1808, his last year at the Pembina post, when grasshoppers ate his entire garden. Grasshoppers have eaten many North Dakota gardens since that time.

LEWIS AND CLARK

Each explorer made a unique contribution to the future state of North Dakota, especially the earliest adventurers who left a permanent written record. But La Vérendrye, David Thompson, and Alexander Henry are not familiar names.

Two men sent by President Thomas Jefferson became better known. Jefferson's secretary-aide, Captain Meriwether Lewis, and Lewis's former commander and friend, Captain William Clark, completed the trip La Vérendrye had dreamed of making. The

Lewis and Clark entering the Mandan Indian village in October 1804

Lewis and Clark Expedition made the 8,000-mile (12,874-kilometer) round-trip passage to the Pacific Ocean. The expedition, which began on the Missouri River near St. Louis on May 14, 1804, and ended September 23, 1806, is one of the most dramatic and significant events in American history. It is unquestionably significant in North Dakota history as well.

Almost four dozen men made the slow journey up the Missouri River against the powerful current. They traveled in two pirogues—canoes made from hollowed tree trunks—and a 55-foot (17-meter) keelboat fitted with one sail. In addition to their clothing, bedding, tools, and cooking utensils, the men carried enormous quantities of beads, medals, flags, dresses, blankets, and other gifts for the Indians they would meet. The trip was a diplomatic as well as a geographic and scientific mission.

Jefferson wanted the men to observe and collect plant, animal, and mineral specimens. They were to record weather data, study native cultures, and conduct tribal councils with the Indians. They also were to keep daily journals.

About five months after leaving St. Louis, the expedition entered North Dakota. On October 23, 1804, they met the Mandans and began to look for winter quarters where they would

Lewis and Clark's original Fort Mandan has been reconstructed on the
Missouri River just west of Washburn.

spend the next five months—the longest they would stay in one
place.

By November 25, the expedition had built Fort Mandan. The
sturdy triangular fort was located near the five Knife River
villages of the friendly Mandan and Hidatsa Indians. Wintering in
North Dakota was valuable for the expedition. Lewis and Clark
made friends among the Indians for the American government.
America had owned this land, part of the mammoth Louisiana
Purchase, only since 1803—shortly before the expedition left
St. Louis. It was important that the Indians be loyal to America,
not to England, Spain, or France, all of whom had previously
claimed American land.

During their stay at Fort Mandan, Lewis and Clark met an
Indian woman who contributed more than any other single
person to the success of the trip. Sakakawea (as North Dakotans

This statue of Lewis and Clark's guide, Sakakawea, stands on the capitol grounds in Bismarck.

spell the more common Sacajawea or Sacagawea) was a Shoshone who had been kidnapped years earlier by the Hidatsas. She became the interpreter, guide, and protector of the Lewis and Clark Expedition.

Sakakawea was the wife of Toussaint Charbonneau, a French-Canadian who was the interpreter for Lewis and Clark at Fort Mandan. The leaders learned that Sakakawea knew the western territory where they would travel; she remembered the land from the time she was captured by the Hidatsas and brought east.

Sakakawea was about sixteen years old when she, Charbonneau, and their newborn son left Fort Mandan with the expedition in April 1805. In an account that reads like a fairy tale, Sakakawea—who carried her infant son on her back—saved both the men and their possessions during their journey to the Pacific. When one of the boats filled with water during a storm,

Sakakawea saved valuable papers, scientific instruments, and the boat itself. When the party needed food, she showed them edible roots, sunflower seeds, wild artichokes, and berries. She also gathered herbs for men who became ill and made ointments for their insect bites and travel sores.

When the party reached Sakakawea's tribal home in Montana, they discovered that her brother was the chief. The relationship ensured that the party would have horses and an escort for the trip across the Rocky Mountains. In November 1805, the Lewis and Clark Expedition reached the Pacific Ocean. Beginning their return journey in March 1806, the group reached their North Dakota starting point in August of that year. Without Sakakawea, historians say, the expedition would have failed.

North Dakota's largest lake is named for Sakakawea, and a bronze statue of her, with her infant son Jean Baptiste in a sacklike carrier on her back, stands on the capitol grounds in Bismarck.

NEW TRADE AND SETTLEMENT

Fur trading formed the foundation for the early plains economy, and it was also an international business. There were some independent traders and trappers in North Dakota, but the British-Canadian and American companies controlled the fur business. Two British-owned companies—the Hudson's Bay Company and its archrival, the North West Company—controlled trade in the Red River Valley.

During the season of 1804-05, more than eleven thousand furs were bought at lower Red River Valley trading posts. But it was not until after the Lewis and Clark Expedition that fur trading gained full momentum in North Dakota, especially along the

A fur traders' camp in buffalo country

Missouri River. The companies were fiercely competitive and sometimes used questionable ethics to keep control of a region. Indian loyalty to traders frequently was bought with liquor.

New American companies were formed. The biggest for many years was John Jacob Astor's American Fur Company. Astor persuaded the American government to pass a law prohibiting other nations from doing business with the Indians.

Manuel Lisa, born in America of Spanish parents, helped to establish the Missouri Fur Company in 1808. Lisa was a natural leader and an excellent trader who managed his own posts. He brought seeds and tools to the Indians, loaned them traps, and gave them the services of his blacksmiths. Lisa's trading posts reached up the Missouri River from Nebraska, through Dakota, and into Montana.

One of the fur-trading posts built by Manuel Lisa (above) along the Missouri River was Fort Manuel (right).

THE SELKIRKERS

The first colony in North Dakota was not very successful, but it was a beginning. The Hudson's Bay Company had given to Thomas Douglas, Earl of Selkirk, an enormous section of land on the Red River of the North. The land extended into North Dakota, Minnesota, and Canada. In 1811, Selkirk attempted to help impoverished Scottish and Irish peasants by bringing them to North America. Intending to keep the Scots and Irish within the British Empire, Selkirk settled the group at Fort Douglas (now Winnipeg), which was Canadian territory in the Red River Valley.

The Selkirkers had neither the tools nor the seeds with which to farm, and they struggled to survive. In addition, they faced hostile employees of the North West Company, who believed that farming would hurt their fur trade. In the fall of 1812, the group headed south, into North Dakota. Abundant herds of buffalo would keep them from starving during the winter of 1812-13.

The Selkirkers built log houses and a protective palisade at Pembina. The settlement was near the trading post established almost a dozen years earlier by Alexander Henry. Movement continued between the Winnipeg settlement of Fort Douglas and

Pembina, the first permanent colony in North Dakota, was established by the Selkirkers in 1812.

Pembina, but gradually the Pembina colony prospered. Métis families also settled at Pembina. Two Catholic missionaries added stability and permanence to the Selkirk colony. In 1818, Father Sévère Dumoulin built a chapel at Pembina. Father Joseph Provencher established a mission near the Selkirk colony at Fort Douglas.

Hostile fur traders, Indian attacks, and crop-killing grasshoppers almost destroyed the Pembina settlement, but new resolve and new colonists kept it alive. A treaty between Great Britain and the United States, however, dealt the final blow to the Pembina colony. When an 1823 survey of the international boundary showed that the Pembina settlement was on the American side of the 49th parallel, the Selkirk colonists moved north to Canada.

THE END OF THE BEGINNING

The first explorers, traders, and settlers had come to northern Dakota. It wasn't North Dakota yet; it wouldn't even be Dakota Territory until 1861. But the beginning was coming to an end. New trade was developing and new people were coming.

Chapter 5
THE PIONEER ERA

THE PIONEER ERA

If North Dakota's growth and development had to be summed
up in six words, they would be *furs, railroads,* and *wheat; courage,*
optimism, and *energy.*

Europeans and Americans in the East wanted furs. Western
America had an abundance. The coveted furs had already brought
trappers, traders, and trading posts to the plains. Furs soon would
play a major part in the development of new transportation as
well.

Once the railroads crossed into Dakota, they would bring tens
of thousands of immigrants, and wheat would be their living. No
pioneer would last long on the vast, lonely land, however,
without enormous quantities of courage, optimism, and energy.

TRADE ROUTES

The fur trade flourished into the 1850s. John Jacob Astor's
American Fur Company built the first steamboat to run on the
upper Missouri River. Christened the *Yellowstone,* the boat could
carry 144 tons (131 metric tons) of goods. It reached Fort Union,
where the Yellowstone and Missouri rivers joined, in 1832.

Other trade routes followed. Ten years after the *Yellowstone*
plied the Missouri, the first Red River cart caravan opened a major
commerce route between St. Paul, Minnesota, and St. Joseph
(now Walhalla), North Dakota. Joseph Rolette, Jr., Norman
Kittson, and Antoine Gingras, three powerful political figures
and traders, ran major fur posts in the St. Joseph-Pembina area.

Steamboat navigation on the Red River, at Fargo

The unique high-wheeled Red River carts, made by the métis entirely of wood, hauled two other basic prairie products besides furs. They carried pemmican and buffalo robes to St. Paul in exchange for manufactured goods. Pemmican, a food that wouldn't spoil and could be carried by traders and hunters, was made from dried, powdered buffalo meat mixed with berries and buffalo fat.

Steamboats didn't come to the Red River until 1859. The *Anson Northrup* was named for the man who accepted a challenge by St. Paul merchants. The St. Paul Chamber of Commerce offered $1,000 to the person who put the first steamboat on the Red River. Northrup demanded and got $2,000 for the small boat he had on the Crow River. He dismantled his boat, and with thirty-two teams of oxen, sixty men, and some sleighs, brought the boat sections to the Red River in the winter of 1859. Reassembled, the

Anson Northrup traveled from Fort Abercrombie to the growing settlement at Fort Garry, near present-day Winnipeg, Canada.

Meanwhile, there were major changes in the Red River Valley. North Dakota's first post office opened at Pembina, where a new permanent agricultural settlement was growing. Leader of the settlement was a saddlemaker from St. Paul named Charles Cavileer.

Father George Anthony Belcourt built Catholic missions at Pembina and St. Joseph. Father Belcourt also established the first flour mill at St. Joseph. In 1853, two Protestants started a mission at St. Joseph. Alonzo Barnard, a Presbyterian, and David B. Spencer, a Congregationalist, gave up their missions, however, after their wives died. One died of "hardship and exposure," and the other was killed by the Sioux.

FROM PRAIRIE TO TERRITORY

The Dakota Territory was created the same year America's Civil War began. President James Buchanan signed the Organic Act on March 2, 1861 "to provide a temporary government for the Territory of Dakota." The status of territory was a preparation for statehood. Not only North and South Dakota but most of Wyoming and Montana were in the original Dakota Territory. Boundaries were redrawn, however, and Wyoming and Montana were removed.

POLITICIANS AND PROMOTERS

Two days after Dakota became a territory, President Abraham Lincoln took office. He appointed his family doctor and campaign manager, Dr. William Jayne, the first territorial governor.

The first home of many North Dakota settlers was a tar-paper shack such as this one. Before winter, sod was stacked up against the outside walls to help keep out the cold and wind.

Writers in the depression-era Federal Writers' Project wrote a comprehensive guide to North Dakota. In the book, they described all ten territorial governors in one way: unpopular with the people. The territorial governors, they said, were "usually from the East and had no interest in the country, their salaries or political advancement being their chief concern."

Other historians judged the governors more kindly, noting that most were honest men who tried to do a good job. One governor, however, did a better job for the railroaders than for the people in his territory. John Burbank, fourth territorial governor, spent much of his time in Washington, D.C., lobbying for special railroad interests. He was made a railroad director but was forced to resign as governor.

NEW LAWS

After creating the Dakota Territory, Congress passed two other bills in the 1860s that pushed open the door to northern Dakota. The first was the Homestead Act of 1862, which gave free land to

The Northern Pacific Railroad reached the Missouri River at Bismarck in 1873.

people who would settle on it and plant crops. Many thousands of homesteaders took advantage of the offer and came to Dakota.

The second bill, passed in 1864, granted a charter to the Northern Pacific Railroad to build a line from Minnesota to the West Coast. Congress gave the company more than 50 million acres (20 million hectares) in Dakota and other northern territories on which to lay track.

The Northern Pacific first entered northern Dakota in 1872, crossing the Red River from Moorhead, Minnesota, to Fargo. The following year, the track reached Bismarck. That year, however, all railroad construction stopped; the money had run out.

One of the country's best known and most successful financiers was Jay Cooke, who had raised funds for the government during the Civil War. It was Cooke's job to raise $100 million for the Northern Pacific. The deal would earn him a handsome profit, including majority ownership in the Northern Pacific Railroad. But selling bonds to put a railroad across the "Great American Desert" was difficult. Not many investors wanted to take a chance on this little-known and little-populated part of the nation. Cooke lost his own fortune and bankrupted his company trying to pay construction costs.

The fall of Jay Cooke and Company triggered the Panic of 1873, a nationwide depression. It took two years and a new railroad president to get the company back on the track and new track on the ground. The Northern Pacific did not complete its run across northern Dakota until 1881.

THE PIONEERS

Nobody rushed to northern Dakota when free land was offered. Beginning January 1, 1863, settlers who promised to cultivate and live on the land could have 160 acres (65 hectares). At the end of five years, they could "prove up" their claim—prove that they had fulfilled the conditions written into the Homestead Act.

It was not until 1868 that Joseph Rolette, Jr., filed the first land claim under the Homestead Act in Dakota. He filed on land in the northern Red River Valley, the only part of northern Dakota that had been surveyed. The 400-mile (644-kilometer) trip to the nearest claim office in Vermillion no doubt put off many a prospective homesteader. During the next couple of years, only about two dozen new claims were filed.

But the 1870s and 1880s were something else. Steamboats, stagecoaches, and ox-drawn wagons had slowly brought settlers to northern Dakota. In 1870, there were 2,405 people living in what would become North Dakota. By 1880, there were almost 37,000 people, and in 1890, there were nearly 191,000.

Tiny towns such as Mott (above) began to spring up when widespread advertising drew settlers to the wide-open lands of North Dakota.

The railroads, anxious for business, and the federal and territorial governments all got into the act to attract newcomers. In addition to free land under the Homestead Act, land was also available under the Timber Culture Act to those who promised to plant a specified number of trees. The Northern Pacific, which had been given almost one-fourth of northern Dakota by Congress, also offered land on easy terms. LAND FOR SALE! was shouted throughout the western world. Promoters played up Dakota's numerous schools and newspapers, its good transportation, fertile soil, and healthful climate. They played down the killer winters.

Territorial officials printed fifty thousand copies of a booklet titled *Dakota* and twenty-five thousand copies of a book called *Resources of Dakota* to push settlement. The Northern Pacific turned a baggage car into a traveling exhibit to show Dakota agricultural products at eastern fairs. In addition, the railroad sent nearly a thousand agents to the British Isles, Norway, Sweden, Denmark, Holland, Switzerland, and Germany to promote the Dakota Territory. It advertised in three hundred American, Canadian, and European newspapers.

The advertising, combined with economic hardship occurring in other nations, did the job. Immigration began in earnest.

Special "immigrant trains" brought thousands of settlers to North Dakota between 1898 and 1915.

Some immigrants continued to come in wagons, but most came by train. The trains also carried the family cattle. Special cars were put on for the animals, furniture, and farm machinery. Author Elwyn B. Robinson tells in his *History of North Dakota* about two Minnesota farmers who filled four cars with "two McCormick wire binders, plows, mowers, harrows, seeders, and sixteen head of horses, as well as four hired men." The pioneers brought everything they could afford to carry in order to build barns, dig wells, chop out sod for houses, plow and plant, and live day by day.

Even after 1900, immigrants continued to come on the special "immigrant trains." North Dakota's population, more than 319,000 in 1900, had grown to 577,000 ten years later. Getting there was hard, but staying was sometimes harder. Summer dust, fall fires, spring floods, winter blizzards, and year-round loneliness bent the bravest. Another problem persisted on the plains: Indian uprisings.

INDIANS AND GOVERNMENT

Who owned the land? Indians, who had lived on the plains longer than recorded history, considered the land their home. The American government and the railroaders wanted the plains for travel routes and settlement.

Government officials attempted to settle the question by treating the tribes like foreign nations: they drew up treaties. They promised payment for lands taken away and moved the Indians to newly created reservations. The government also established military forts to protect travelers and settlers from Indians who were angry at being confined and forced into a non-Indian lifestyle. Fort Abercrombie, built on the Red River in 1857, was the first in northern Dakota. Within a few years, there were almost a dozen more, including Fort Rice, built in 1864 on the Missouri River.

History would have been written differently if Indian agents, army officers, and other government officials had not violated the treaties. The worst violation in North Dakota involved the Laramie Treaty with the Teton Sioux, signed in 1868.

The Sioux were given a 22-million-acre (9-million-hectare) reservation that included land in both northern and southern Dakota. The present Standing Rock Reservation in the southern part of North Dakota was part of the agreement. The Sioux were also promised daily food provisions of meat and flour, plus horses, oxen, and farm equipment. Teachers, doctors, and blacksmiths were to be provided. The Indians would be allowed to hunt buffalo to the west of the reservation, and white people would not be allowed on the reservation without permission.

Within a few years, however, railroads sent surveyors — accompanied by army units — onto Standing Rock Reservation.

Between 1867 and 1882, the federal government moved North Dakota's Indians to reservations: Mandans, Hidatsas, and Arikaras to the Fort Berthold Indian Reservation; Devils Lake Sioux to Fort Totten (above); Turtle Mountain Chippewas to Turtle Mountain (left); and Standing Rock Sioux to Standing Rock (below).

George Armstrong Custer, then a lieutenant colonel, led a military expedition through the Black Hills in southern Dakota, also part of the Sioux reservation. When word spread that there was gold in the Black Hills, the federal government allowed thousands of gold-seekers to enter Indian land. The government urged the Sioux to sell the Black Hills, but they refused.

White Indian agents, responsible for providing the food promised by the government, sold it elsewhere. The consequences of these breaches of the Laramie Treaty were devastating and permanent. Many Sioux, no longer trusting the white man, left the reservation. General Custer and his entire command were killed by the Sioux in the Battle of the Little Big Horn. The Sioux won a battle, but the United States government won the war. The Indians were forced to stay on their reservations, learn to farm, and try to adapt to a white civilization. The government also took the Black Hills from the Indians, paying them nothing.

BONANZA FARMS

Not until after 1870 did wheat make a big impact on the Dakota economy. In that year, two Minnesotans developed a new milling process for spring wheat. This was a northern crop that was planted in the spring when the ground was thawed and harvested in the fall before it froze. In the new process, called the ''Minnesota patent,'' rollers instead of mill stones were used to grind the wheat and a purifier was used to separate the bran from the flour. For the first time, white flour made from spring wheat was considered superior to flour made from winter wheat. Spring wheat was launched as the main crop of the northern plains.

Railroaders became ''bonanza farmers'' and began to grow wheat. When the Panic of 1873 occurred, the Northern Pacific

Dozens of horse-drawn plows were needed to till the acreage of the huge Bagg bonanza farm in Richland County.

sold some of its land. John B. Power, land agent for the Northern Pacific, convinced railroad president George W. Cass and a director, Benjamin Cheney, to buy more than 13,000 acres (5,261 hectares) in the Red River Valley and begin the first bonanza farm. If such a venture were successful, Power reasoned, the entire nation would take note and new settlers would come to Dakota.

The entire nation did take note. The Cass and Cheney farm, managed by a lawyer and former Minnesota farmer named Oliver Dalrymple, was hugely successful. Magazines ran articles about the bonanza farms, and President Rutherford B. Hayes visited the Cass-Cheney-Dalrymple farm. Within about ten years, there were ninety huge bonanza farms. Most of them were owned by businessmen interested in making money. Farm managers, superintendents, and foremen ran the operations like factories. Thousands of new settlers came to work on the mammoth farms or start their own smaller spreads.

Bonanza farming showed the country what could be done on the Dakota plains, but the boom did not last. The success of the farms had driven up land prices to such an extent that many owners decided to sell so they could realize huge profits. The owners were also aware that a dry North Dakota summer could wipe out the profits they had already earned. In 1890, a nationwide depression caused wheat prices to plummet. Most of

In 1883, the Marquis de Mores and his wife (left) settled on the Little Missouri River. The marquis built a twenty-six-room château (above) as well as a town named Medora in honor of his wife.

the big farms, for these reasons and others, were broken up and sold. But even without the big operations, North Dakota farming was ahead of that in some other states.

THE BEEF BONANZA

In the early 1800s, a United States Army general named James S. Brisbin wrote a book with a great sales pitch: *The Beef Bonanza; or, How to Get Rich on the Plains.* "The plains of America" was one of only five great natural grazing areas in the world, according to Brisbin, and he said that enormous profits could be made by investing in cattle. The book brought new cattle ranchers to North Dakota in the 1880s. The Badlands, in particular, became well known as a cattle-grazing region.

The challenge of the West and a chance to get rich in the cattle business drew an ambitious young Frenchman, the Marquis de Mores, to North Dakota. The marquis and his wife, a New Yorker named Medora, came to the Badlands in 1883. They settled on the

This cabin on the Maltese Cross Ranch was Teddy Roosevelt's North Dakota headquarters.

east side of the Little Missouri River, where they would soon build a town.

The marquis planned to revolutionize the beef industry. He thought it would be smarter to slaughter cattle on the range and send the dressed beef to market in the East rather than to ship live herds. He built a $250,000 packing plant, a twenty-six-room château, and a few buildings in the town. Within a year, the new boomtown had eighty-four buildings. But the boom was short-lived. The marquis, who had thousands of cattle and sheep, a horse-breeding operation, a stagecoach line into the Black Hills, and a payroll to meet, was overextended. His businesses in the town died. More than a million dollars in debt, the Marquis de Mores returned to France in 1886.

The open-range cattle industry in general suffered in the Little Missouri grassland region. Drought and grasshoppers reduced the supply of grass for grazing in the summer of 1886. That fall, fire burned off more of the grass, and early deep snows covered the rest. Cattle companies pulled out. One rancher who was especially discouraged at the losses on the range was Teddy Roosevelt. In 1883, the young Roosevelt had bought the Maltese Cross Ranch, a few miles south of Medora, and later the Elkhorn Ranch, about 35 miles (56 kilometers) north of the town.

DAKOTA DIVIDED: STATEHOOD

North Dakotans have always been politically aware, and from the start, they have enjoyed a good political battle. They tired of being controlled from Washington, D.C., by leaders whose special interests came ahead of the people. One of the master politicians of the period was Alexander McKenzie. Although he held only one elected office in his lifetime—that of sheriff—McKenzie became the political boss of northern Dakota.

A Northern Pacific employee, McKenzie protected the financial interests of the railroad, the banks, and lumber and insurance companies by influencing legislation to make or save money for the businesses. Territorial Governor Nehemiah Ordway, another man of questionable ethics, was a friend of McKenzie. Both Ordway and McKenzie influenced legislation that led to moving the territorial capital from Yankton, in the south, to Bismarck, in McKenzie's Burleigh County. Governor Ordway, accused of accepting a bribe to move the capital, was removed from office after protests by the citizens.

During the 1880s, several efforts were made by territorial residents to admit Dakota to the Union. Conventions were held and bills were introduced in Congress. None was successful. Special-interest groups, notably the railroads and flour mills, opposed statehood. They wanted to keep a territorial government that looked after their interests.

In 1887, the territorial legislature requested that a vote be taken on the issue of splitting the territory and making two states. Voters said yes, but by a narrow margin. Both parts of the

A constitutional convention parade was held in Bismarck on July 4, 1889.

territory had far exceeded the usual population for becoming a state. Northern Dakota had more than 190,000 residents and southern Dakota more than 348,000; only 60,000 were required for statehood.

Early in 1889, Congress passed the Omnibus Bill, which authorized the drafting of constitutions for North Dakota, South Dakota, Montana, and Washington. Delegates were elected and constitutional conventions were called. North Dakota's constitutional convention convened on July 4, 1889. The delegates hammered out the original twenty articles in forty-five days. In October, voters approved the new constitution by a vote of more than three to one.

President Benjamin Harrison signed the documents making North Dakota and South Dakota two states on November 2, 1889. He never knew which document he signed first. Born of one territory, he considered the states "twins," and he covered the names while signing. As a result, both states claim to be thirty-ninth. Officially, North Dakota—the first alphabetically—is considered the thirty-ninth state to be admitted to the Union, South Dakota the fortieth.

Chapter 6
A NEW DESTINY

A NEW DESTINY

When North Dakota was granted statehood, the North Dakota pioneers gained some much-desired control over their own destiny. For the first time, they could elect a governor. They could also loosen the grip that Boss McKenzie, the railroads, and the grain merchants had on their lives.

THE FIRST STATE GOVERNMENT

North Dakotans were certain that the new constitution would pass and that they would be granted statehood almost immediately. They were so certain, in fact, that they elected their state officials at the same time they approved the constitution, on October 1, 1889. When President Harrison declared statehood on November 2, 1889, North Dakota was ready. John Miller, a successful farmer and land speculator from Richland County, was the first governor.

The first legislative assembly, which convened November 19, 1889, had to organize not only state government but county and city government as well. It passed laws regulating railroads and grain businesses, and it selected the state's first United States senators.

The years between 1900 and World War I were "swing years" for North Dakota. It was swinging over—slowly—from pioneering to solid statehood and a more stable farm economy.

The Northern Pacific Railroad station in Bismarck

Railroads expanded and branch lines served most towns. The state had more track in proportion to its population than any other state in the country. Farmers got good prices for their crops, and the population rose rapidly.

Three more things happened to give North Dakota status and strength: the defeat of Alexander McKenzie as political boss, the growth of cooperatives, and the formation of the Nonpartisan League. Reform candidate John Burke was elected governor in 1906, beating the incumbent McKenzie machine candidate. Two years later, McKenzie gave up another power base when he resigned as Republican party national chairman. The voters, ready for widespread reform, elected Burke governor for three terms.

New laws were passed to curb favors from railroaders to legislators. Legislators attempted to end corrupt election practices and improve the courts. They passed a law creating the direct primary election, in which the voters, not the machine bosses, would pick the candidates. Reformers also campaigned against labor abuses, especially those involving children and farm workers.

Burke's influence continued long after his three terms of office, and went far beyond North Dakota. He became treasurer of the United States and a justice of the North Dakota Supreme Court. A statue of John Burke is in the Capitol at Washington, D.C. He is the only North Dakotan to have this honor.

THE NONPARTISAN LEAGUE

North Dakota wheat farmers felt that too many middlemen took a profit between farm and flour mill, depriving farmers of a fair share. They believed that weighing and grading practices were unfair and that transportation and storage costs were too high. During the early 1900s, farmers tried to gain more control over the marketing of their wheat by forming farmers' associations called cooperatives. Farmers who were members of the cooperatives worked together to try to get fair market prices for their wheat. The cooperatives did help to stem the abuses, but on the whole were not very successful in attaining their goals.

A former farmer who blamed his financial ruin on market speculators began a major movement that left a permanent mark on North Dakota agriculture. Arthur C. Townley decided that a large and powerful farmers' organization was needed. The result was the Nonpartisan League (NPL). Townley was a highly successful organizer, and within a year the NPL had forty thousand members. The NPL platform called for numerous state-owned businesses and services to help the struggling farmers. State-owned terminal elevators, state-owned banks that gave low-interest loans, and state grain inspectors who maintained uniform

Arthur C. Townley, organizer of the Nonpartisan League, speaking at a farmers' rally

standards were part of the plan. State hail insurance against crop loss was another proposal.

People opposed to "state socialism" in the form of the NPL established the Independent Voters' Association (IVA). But the NPL had the backing of enough voters to gain state leadership positions. In 1918, NPL candidates captured every state office but one. Over the years, five Nonpartisan League candidates became governor, although they are sometimes listed as Republicans. Considered a farmers' organization and not a political party in spite of its intense political activities, the NPL candidates were listed in the Republican column on ballots.

Ironically, a constitutional amendment introduced by the NPL was used against the organization to oust its first governor. The amendment permitted the voters to recall an elected official by a special election. In 1921, the IVA used the recall not only against

The State Bank of North Dakota, established in 1919, is still in operation.

NPL Governor Lynn J. Frazier but also against the attorney general and the commissioner of agriculture. Until 1988, when Arizona recalled Governor Evan Mecham, North Dakota was the only state to recall its governor.

Although NPL candidates would continue to be elected to state office into the 1930s, the League's strength was declining. In 1956, a reorganized and much tamer Nonpartisan League merged with the Democratic party.

The Nonpartisan League left its mark on the state, and today many of its socialistic ideas would not raise an eyebrow among voters. Reform measures under NPL leadership included tax breaks for farmers, additional money for schools, and an improved system for grading grain. Two state-owned businesses—unique in the nation—still operate: the Bank of North Dakota at Bismarck and the State Mill and Elevator at Grand Forks.

During the drought of the 1930s, winds blew the dry topsoil away and created sand dunes where crops once had thrived.

Reform movements did not solve all of North Dakota's problems. Indeed, the economy became so bad in the 1920s with bank closings and in the 1930s with drought and depression, that thousands of people left the state to find work. North Dakota, nonetheless, had proved that it could look after its own and would continue to shape its own destiny.

A PRESIDENTIAL CANDIDATE

In 1936, a third national party appeared in opposition to the established Republican and Democratic parties. Members of the Union party wanted to defeat Franklin D. Roosevelt, who was running for president on the Democratic ticket. The Union party's Republican opposition was Alf Landon.

United States Congressman William Lemke, from North Dakota, was nominated as the Union party candidate for president. The one-time NPL attorney general, who had been recalled in 1921, received less than 1 million votes and did not carry any state. But Lemke did win the distinction of being the only presidential candidate to come from North Dakota.

THE POST-DEPRESSION YEARS

Wounds from the Great Depression and Dust Bowl years were deep, and they left permanent scars on the face of North Dakota. Population dropped by nearly 39,000 in the 1930s and by more than 22,000 in the 1940s.

Two significant events in the 1940s and 1950s helped the struggling agricultural state heal its economic wounds and rebuild its population. One was the Pick-Sloan Plan, approved by the United States Congress in 1944 to develop the Missouri River basin. North Dakota's Garrison Dam, part of Pick-Sloan, would relieve flooding along the Missouri, produce hydroelectricity from five generators, and help farmers irrigate their land. It would be one of the largest earthen dams in the world; its reservoir, Lake Sakakawea, would be the largest artificially created lake entirely within one state. The dam, begun in 1946, was completed in 1954. The first electric power was generated in January 1956.

The second event was the discovery of oil near Tioga. Oil companies had drilled in western North Dakota for decades before oil was discovered on the Clarence Iverson farm in 1951. In fact, the legislative assembly had anticipated an oil boom. In 1941, legislators repealed outdated laws and passed new ones related to oil production.

Oil companies, prospectors, and wildcatters swarmed into the Williston oil basin. Many were successful. Although production dropped in the late 1960s and early 1970s, a new boom began in

The Garrison Dam power plant

the late 1970s when new locations were discovered. Oil brought
new money to the state, but it also caused crowded schools,
housing shortages, and crime. Many North Dakotans considered
the new prosperity a mixed blessing. But by the end of the 1980s,
both the prosperity and the problems it brought had almost
disappeared. Oil prices and oil production had plunged.

THE GARRISON DIVERSION PROJECT

A long-standing controversy in North Dakota centers on the
Garrison Diversion Project. Even before statehood, many North
Dakotans wanted a plan to divert water from the Missouri River
to irrigate crops. Although Garrison Dam was completed in 1954,
it was not until 1965 that Congress funded the diversion project.

A vast network of pumping stations, canals, reservoirs, and pipelines was part of the long-term plans.

Several features were finished before the United States Department of the Interior reexamined the controversial Garrison Diversion Project in 1977. Completion was put on hold. Proponents of the plan argue that it will bring needed water to farms for crops and to cities that have water shortages. It will develop new recreation and wildlife areas and boost the state's economy by millions of dollars.

Opponents of the plan, however, say it will reduce cropland and grassland, reduce needed wetlands for migratory birds, and harm wild animals by changing their natural habitat. They also say that irrigation runoff will pollute the rivers into which it flows and that the project cost will be more than the monetary benefits in the long run. The controversy continues, not only in North Dakota but nationwide and in Canada, which shares rivers with North Dakota.

COMPUTERS: FARM EQUIPMENT FOR THE 1990s

Computers may become as important to farming as they are to business and manufacturing. One of the biggest challenges facing the farmer each year is deciding what can be grown most profitably. The solution: a computer program that tells the farmer what to grow.

The *Bismarck Tribune* reported in 1988 that economists at the North Dakota State University Extension were testing a computer program to help the farmer figure costs, profits, government restrictions, and other variables for the best combination of grain crops. Next, the economists plan to develop expanded software that includes livestock and more-complex crops.

Chapter 7
GOVERNMENT
AND THE ECONOMY

GOVERNMENT AND THE ECONOMY

All political power is inherent in the people.
Government is instituted for the protection, security
and benefit of the people, and they have a right to alter
or reform the same whenever the public good may require.
—Article I, Section 2, Constitution of North Dakota

GOVERNMENT

The government of North Dakota, like the government of the
United States, is divided into three branches: the legislative, which
makes the laws; the executive, which carries out the laws; and the
judicial, which interprets the laws.

The state senate and house of representatives make up the
Legislative Assembly. The assembly consists of 106 representatives
and 53 state senators. House members serve two-year terms and
senators serve four-year terms. Senate elections, however, like
house elections, occur every two years. Senators from odd-
numbered districts are elected one time, those from even-
numbered districts the next. The rotation of senate elections helps
the assembly maintain continuity and experience.

A new session of the assembly begins every two years. The
assembly convenes in January following the fall election of all
house members and half the senate. Legislators may meet at any
time during the two-year period, or biennium, but not more than

a total of eighty days. Special sessions called by the governor do not count as part of the eighty days. Eighty days out of two years seems like a short time to pass laws and resolutions, oversee state spending, help constituents, and approve appointments. Legislators consider almost one thousand bills—prospective laws—in each biennium. Much of the work, however, is handled by legislative committees not bound by the eighty-day constitutional limit. Many state legislators have other jobs that would be jeopardized by a longer session.

A relatively modern addition to North Dakota government is the legislative council. The council, formed in 1945, makes it possible for the assembly to handle an increasing workload and remain a part-time citizen legislature. The council consists of fifteen senators and representatives, including the majority and minority leaders of both houses and the speaker of the house. Their primary purpose is to direct studies requested by the assembly. These studies are carried out by legislative committees and a staff of attorneys, accountants, researchers, and office personnel. Some council accomplishments include the revision of inadequate or outdated school, election, criminal, and motor-vehicle laws.

The governor is the chief executive of the state. A constitutional amendment, adopted in 1964, increased the term of the governor from two years to four. Since 1976, the governor and lieutenant governor have been on the same party ballot, and voters cast one vote for the two candidates. The governor of North Dakota is commander-in-chief of the state militia. The chief executive prepares the budget for all state services and programs. When necessary, he calls special sessions of the Legislative Assembly. He also may grant reprieves and pardons to prisoners and may sign or veto legislation.

Although the governor is the chief executive of the state, North Dakota's decentralized government gives other officials authority over their departments. This provides safeguards against a chief executive wielding too much power. There are twelve elected officials in addition to the governor and lieutenant governor, and appointed officials head dozens of agencies, boards, and commissions. Some North Dakotans feel that it is too large and costly a government.

The judicial branch hears and decides civil and criminal cases. For a number of years, North Dakota has been reorganizing its court system so it will operate more efficiently and fairly. The judicial article of the state constitution was rewritten to provide for a unified court system in which the state supreme court guides and directs the lower courts. The highest court is the supreme court, which consists of five justices elected on a nonpartisan, or "no-party," ballot for ten-year terms. The five justices appoint a chief justice from their membership. The state is divided into seven judicial districts, and the assembly decides how many judges are needed. District judges are elected for six-year terms. There are also county and municipal courts, which are limited as to the type of case they hear.

INCOME AND EXPENSES

The governor, with the help of the budget director, state agencies, and legislators, prepares a two-year budget. The 1987-89 biennial budget was between $2 billion and $3 billion. Of that amount, almost $900 million was earmarked for education and almost $700 million for health and welfare programs. State parks, police, highways, agriculture, and industry added millions more to the budget. North Dakota spends billions of dollars less each

By 1988, only a dozen one-room schools were left in North Dakota.

year than states with bigger populations, such as Illinois and New York. But even $1 billion is a high price for a state with fewer than 700,000 people.

Taxes are North Dakota's most important source of income. The sales tax brings more than $500 million to the state over a two-year period. Two other major sources of state tax revenue are income taxes and severance taxes. A severance tax refers to severing, or taking, minerals from the soil. North Dakota has three kinds of severance taxes involving oil and gas production, oil extraction, and coal severance. Several lesser taxes, fees for services, and federal grants also provide state income.

EDUCATION

Many North Dakota pioneers were well educated for their era when they settled on the prairie. But paying for quality education in the sparsely populated state has been a continuing struggle. In 1920, there were some five thousand one-room rural schools in North Dakota. Salaries of rural teachers were among the lowest in the nation, and some teachers had not even completed high school. After World War II, hundreds of school districts were reorganized and rural schools were consolidated into larger, graded schools. Consolidation resulted in better-qualified teachers, better equipment, and more-advanced course offerings. By 1988, there were only a dozen one-room rural schools left, with fewer than a hundred students altogether. Many of the smaller schools are now utilizing satellite-based education programs.

The superintendent of public instruction, elected to a four-year term, oversees all public elementary and high schools in the state. County and district superintendents have the direct responsibility for schools in their area. At the end of the 1980s, there were 310 public school districts.

In addition to the public primary and secondary schools, there are more than a hundred parochial and private schools in the state. There are also elementary and high schools run by the federal Bureau of Indian Affairs. Total enrollment in all North Dakota schools is about 128,000.

There are six state universities in North Dakota. The University of North Dakota was created in 1883 at Grand Forks when Nehemiah Ordway, governor of the Dakota Territory, signed "enabling" legislation into law. There were four faculty members and eleven students on opening day in 1884. Today, there is also a UND extension at Williston. North Dakota State University of Agricultural and Applied Science—first called North Dakota Agricultural College—was established by the first state legislature in 1890, at Fargo. Also part of the university is the two-year State School of Forestry-Bottineau Branch.

Students at the United Tribes Technical College in Bismarck

In addition to training students for many professions, UND and NDSU play important roles in the state's two top economic activities: agriculture and mining. NDSU does extensive agricultural research and has branch agricultural research centers in Dickinson, Williston, Hettinger, Minot, Langdon, Carrington, Streeter, and Mandan. There is also an agronomy seed farm at Casselton. The university's Agricultural Experiment Station investigates, tests, and reports findings for all types of problems that relate to agriculture and farm life. UND carries out research on energy, mining, and mineral resources.

Other state universities are at Dickinson, Mayville, Minot, and Valley City. The Enabling Act of 1889, which paved the way for dividing the Dakota Territory into North and South Dakota and enabled the people to form governments, also provided land grants for normal schools (teacher training colleges). Valley City State University originally was a land-grant normal school. Mayville and Minot also began as normal schools.

The old engineering building at North Dakota State University (left) and the modern Center for Aerospace Science at the University of North Dakota (above)

There are also five state-supported two-year institutions in North Dakota: four state-supported community colleges (NDSU-Bottineau, UND-Lake Region at Devils Lake, UND-Williston, and Bismarck State College) and the two-year State College of Science, at Wahpeton. Four tribal community colleges are located at Fort Berthold, Turtle Mountain, Fort Totten, and Standing Rock Indian reservations. Private colleges include the University of Mary, at Bismarck; Jamestown College, at Jamestown; and Trinity Bible Institute, at Ellendale.

AGRICULTURE

"When tillage begins, other arts follow. The farmers therefore are the founders of human civilization," said statesman Daniel Webster more than a century ago.

Fur trading, not farming, came first in North Dakota. But farming was definitely the beginning of civilization in that state. It

Though wheat (right) is still North Dakota's main cash crop, the state ranks first in the production of sunflowers (above).

is still the backbone of the economy and the dominant factor in the lifestyle of all North Dakotans, including city dwellers.

"King wheat" built North Dakota; for decades it was the only major cash crop. Chances are, when you eat spaghetti and other pasta products, you're eating North Dakota-grown durum. In 1987, North Dakota ranked first in the nation in production of durum and other spring wheat, producing 80 percent of all durum raised in the country.

Wheat is still king, but it is no longer absolute monarch. Other crops grown in North Dakota make up more than half of the cash receipts at market time. The state ranks first not only in spring wheat but also in flaxseed, sunflowers, barley, pinto beans, and rye. Fields of tall, yellow-petaled sunflowers are grown in every North Dakota county, and in 1987, the state produced 80 percent

Though most of North Dakota's beef cattle are raised in the west, these Hereford cows and calves (above) are grazing in a pasture near Ludden.

of all sunflowers nationwide. Some are grown for the edible seeds, some for the oil. Sugar beets are also a major crop, providing much of the nation's sugar supply.

Livestock earn a large income for North Dakota—almost $800 million in the late 1980s. The higher, drier west, more suited to cattle than to crops, is ranch country. This is where most of the state's beef cattle are raised and fattened for market. Livestock also includes sheep, hogs, poultry—and bees! North Dakota ranks second in the country in honey production. More than meat comes from the so-called meat animals. Dairy products, eggs, and wool boost livestock income.

In 1900, an average farm had 343 acres (139 hectares); in 1987, the average size was 1,252 acres (507 hectares). Consequently, the number of farms has dropped from an all-time high of 84,605 in

Coal (above) and oil (right) are the most important minerals mined in North Dakota.

1935 to 32,500 in 1987. Modern equipment, designed to help farmers, has instead helped to put many farmers out of business. The price tags were too high and the profits were too low for them to survive. The farmers and ranchers who have lasted usually have expanded slowly, bought carefully, and avoided major debt.

MINING

In addition to its exceptionally fertile soil, North Dakota has some of the richest, most abundant mineral reserves in the world. Clay, which is easily mined, is made into bricks and ceramic products in the western part of the state. Salt is mined from several beds and processed for livestock feed, oil-drilling operations, and use in water softeners. Glacial sand and gravel are used to maintain roads. Before hard surfaces were put on the main highways, local sand and gravel were used to build the roads.

Leading the list of minerals, of course, are oil and lignite coal. These have made North Dakota's energy-related industries second only to agriculture. More than ten thousand North Dakotans earn their living in the oil industry. They work in bulk storage operations, service stations, crude oil and gas production, refining, and pipeline transportation.

Coal mining has caused controversy in recent years. In the early days, coal was dug crudely from the hills for fuel supplies. But mining began in earnest when the Northern Pacific Railroad opened several lignite mines along its tracks in 1884, five years before North Dakota became a state. The first large mine was opened in Washburn, near the Missouri River, in 1900.

North Dakota's brownish-black lignite is called second-stage coal. It is older and more compressed than peat but younger and softer than bituminous or anthracite. Unlike hard coal, lignite veins are near the surface and can be surface-mined without deep tunnels. There are an estimated 350 billion tons (318 billion metric tons) of lignite in the state, and about 15 billion tons (14 billion metric tons) are mineable.

The lignite provides vast electric power—and employment— through eight generating plants in western North Dakota. Mining itself provides additional and much-needed jobs. Like the oil industry, coal mining is a mixed blessing. Enormously important to the economy, coal mining has also scarred the landscape. This is an important consideration to North Dakotans who value the beauty of their land. Huge shovels and draglines remove the earth that covers the veins of coal and drop it to form ridges. Although some of the ridges—called spoil banks or spoil piles—have been reclaimed with topsoil and new plantings, the scars remain.

This plant in West Fargo produces sunflower oil, linseed oil, and soybean oil.

BUSINESS AND INDUSTRY

Fargo, Grand Forks, Bismarck, Minot, and the other large cities have the usual assortment of businesses. Retail stores, real estate offices, banks, car and truck dealerships, restaurants, dry cleaners, and hair stylists are in or near most towns. Modern malls stock merchandise similar to their counterparts elsewhere in the nation.

Fargo, the largest city and home of North Dakota State University, is the most diversified. Bismarck, the state capital, has the nation's only state-owned bank, the Bank of North Dakota.

Grand Forks and Minot have an added distinction. Each city has a military air base that puts dollars into the local economy. Military employees purchase goods in the area, and the military bases also hire local civilians.

Tanker refueling planes and bombers are stationed at both Strategic Air Command (SAC) bases. The new B2 bombers are stationed at Grand Forks. The Grand Forks facility is also the launch-control site for intercontinental ballistic missiles (ICBMs). Minuteman missiles are stored in protective silos that are buried in the earth at several locations. It is said unofficially but openly that North Dakota would be the third- or fourth-strongest nuclear power in the world if it were a nation instead of a state.

Most manufacturing in North Dakota is related to agriculture. In 1851, missionary-priest Father George A. Belcourt built the state's first flour mill at Walhalla. Today's companies still produce flour, as well as potato chips, flakes for instant mashed potatoes, honey, table sugar, and sunflower oil. The only state-owned mill and elevator for making flour and storing grain is located in Grand Forks.

Other plants make fertilizer, farm machinery, and specialized equipment. Huge tractors are made in Fargo at the Steiger Tractor Manufacturing Plant. Melrose Division of Clark Equipment Company, known internationally for its Bobcat tractors, also makes farm equipment in North Dakota.

An unusual manufacturing operation that's not associated with agriculture is located at Rolla. The William Langer Jewel Bearing Plant makes bearings for military use from synthetic rubies and sapphires. The tiny jewels—traditionally used in watches—are also used in bombsights, range finders, and other military instruments. The Rolla plant is operated by Bulova for the United States government.

Chapter 8
RECREATION AND LEISURE

RECREATION AND LEISURE

We would dance all night. Everybody—Bohemians, Norwegians—
it didn't matter what they were, we just went and had a good time.
—from *Sods, Logs, & Tar-paper*, an oral history

North Dakota has an advantage over some older states. Still living in the state are pioneers who remember settling on the virgin prairie with their parents when the state was only fifteen or twenty years old.

Recreation in those early days was a family affair. "I had seven brothers and six sisters and we had our own musical instruments," eighty-nine-year-old Hilda Bohlin recalled for the oral history put together in 1988 by the North Dakota Extension Homemakers' Council. "My dad used to go out Saturday nights and play the accordion for dances. We had a musical family, all except me. I had to wash dishes."

Parents and children have more separate activities today, but North Dakota festivals, powwows, concerts, and sports still include all ages. A listing of more than four hundred events in the state includes a demolition derby, an overnight sailboat race, a Boy Scout Jamboree, a jazz festival, and dogsled races.

OUTDOOR RECREATION

Just a few generations ago, settlers struggled so they would have a warm, comfortable house in which to live. Now, thousands of North Dakotans leave the comforts of home to hunt, fish, camp, and play in the snow.

Fishing is a popular year-round activity for North Dakota outdoor enthusiasts.

More than 100,000 residents held hunting licenses in one recent season, and almost 162,000 held fishing licenses. Newspapers announce the opening of the mourning dove, beaver, and coyote hunting seasons. Sportsmen also watch for the opening of duck, turkey, goose, raccoon, fox, and badger seasons. Peak time for salmon fishing is front-page news in the *Bismarck Tribune*. Lake Sakakawea, North Dakota's largest lake, is described as one of the best lunker walleye lakes around. Each year about two hundred two-man teams compete in the Governor's Cup Walleye Fishing Tournament. Jet-skiers, sailors, swimmers, and scuba divers also use Lake Sakakawea.

Scores of spectators watch the annual Great American Horse Race held in September at Fort Abraham Lincoln State Park, near Mandan. Inspired by the first pony-express riders, modern riders race their sure-footed mounts over rugged terrain for a cash prize.

The state's legendary cold winter weather brings out the skaters, skiers, and snowmobilers. Some of the hardiest winter-sports enthusiasts compete in the Regina (Canada)-Minot International

Centennial festivities drew thousands
of visitors during the summer of 1989.

250 Snowmobile Cross-Country Race. The 250-mile (402-
kilometer) race is billed as the longest true cross-country
snowmobile adventure on the North American continent.

SPORTS

There are no professional sports teams in North Dakota. Many
fans of professional sports cheer on the neighboring Minnesota
Vikings during football season and the Minnesota Twins during
baseball season. But college and high-school sports are covered by
local radio and television. The spirited annual state basketball
tournaments for the boys "A" and "B" leagues are popular sports
events in the state. Hockey is a popular sport in eastern North
Dakota. UND's Division I hockey team has won three national
championships. The Prairie Rose State Games, patterned after the
Olympics, began in 1987 to promote amateur athletics.

A bicycle race is one of the events included in the Prairie Rose State Games.

FESTIVALS

Old times, modern times, farm life, Native American heritage, and European cultures are celebrated annually in North Dakota. One of the newest festivals is Pastaville, USA, created to acknowledge North Dakota farmers who produce most of the nation's durum wheat, the main ingredient of pasta.

Potato Bowl USA, with a football game, a parade, and a queen contest, salutes another major cash crop each September at Grand Forks. Towns all over the state celebrate their Norwegian, Swedish, Danish, and Icelandic heritages with Scandinavian festivals throughout the year.

Norwegian royalty attends the annual Scandinavian Festival at Fargo. And in Bismarck each year, Native Americans hold the United Tribes Powwow with singing and dancing competitions.

Every July, Grand Forks returns in spirit to the 1890s, when the Red River was a major transportation route. Riverboat Days recall the history of "the Forks" and feature old-time entertainment such as frog-jumping contests, log rolling, canoe races, and rolling-pin tosses.

VISUAL AND PERFORMING ARTS

North Dakota artists, musicians, and performers get little recognition compared with those in more populated states. But the arts are expanding in the Flickertail State. In 1988, a theater group called Dakota Stage Ltd. celebrated its tenth anniversary by moving into its first permanent home. It occupies the Gem, Bismarck's oldest theater, which was built in 1905. The Gem is on the National Register of Historic Places.

American Indian art has become increasingly popular, and the North Dakota Indian Arts Association hopes to bring more Native American art to the state. It also wants to keep its talented artists from leaving the state, as many have done. Association members are planning a long-range dream: a Native American Arts and Cultural Center in Mandan.

Three groups have given North Dakota artists and audiences their biggest boost. One is the North Dakota Council on the Arts, created by the legislature in 1967. The second is the National Endowment for the Arts, signed into law by President Lyndon B. Johnson two years earlier. The National Endowment for the Arts grants money to school and community art projects in all states. The third is the North Dakota Humanities Council, an affiliate of the National Endowment for the Humanities.

In less than twenty years, small towns as well as major cities in North Dakota were receiving federal and state money for the arts and humanities—and raising their own money locally as well. By 1987, artists representing all the visual, performing, and communications arts had received fellowships. The final art form to be recognized with a fellowship from the North Dakota Council on the Arts was filmmaking.

THE COWBOY POETS

A few years ago, western folklorists rediscovered an old art form: cowboy poetry. Nobody needed entertainment and a chance to "let down" more than cowboys after a long trail ride. Alone on the prairie, the men entertained each other with poems, stories, and songs about their work. They sat around the campfire and wove stories based on humor and hardships. Some of the poems had hundreds of verses. Part of the art was in the telling, voice rising and falling, pausing and racing, to create a mood.

A hundred years or so after its peak on the western plains, cowboy poetry is being resurrected. The first national gathering of modern cowboy poets was held at Elko, Nevada, in 1985. The annual gatherings have drawn as many as ten thousand listeners.

In 1987, in an event sponsored by the North Dakota Humanities Council, men and women gathered on Memorial Day weekend at Medora for North Dakota's first cowboy poetry telling. Annual "reunions" have followed. One of North Dakota's most talented cowboy poets, Bill Lowman, helped to begin the Medora event.

Not all cowboy poets have been men. Wives and mothers knew something about cowboy life in the late 1800s and early 1900s. One woman poet who had lived in the Badlands since 1902 also wrote about riding. Her daughters read her work at Medora.

As one North Dakota pioneer said of her early days, "We had hard times, but we had fun, too."

Chapter 9

HIGHLIGHTS OF THE FLICKERTAIL STATE

HIGHLIGHTS OF THE FLICKERTAIL STATE

*Discover the spirit! The spirit of North Dakota
is like nothing you've ever felt. It's a spirit
of timelessness and adventure that makes the past
come alive and gives new excitement to the present.*
—North Dakota Tour Brochure

After struggling to build a state on the windblown prairie, North Dakotans are taking a good look at their successes. They are also inviting others to do the same.

North Dakota is not for people who are in a hurry. The highways are flat, fast, and generally uncrowded, but some cities and sites are more than 100 miles (161 kilometers) apart. Those who speed through the state run the risk of missing some unmarked treasures.

One way to see North Dakota is to divide it into sections. Wide-open Rough Rider Country is in the far west. The Red River Valley, with more cities and a midwestern flavor, is on the state's historic eastern boundary. Peace Garden Country is on the Canadian border, and the Prairie Heartland is south of Peace Garden Country and west of the Red River Valley region. The Missouri River Corridor runs through the middle of the state. Each can be sampled briefly or exhaustively; each has a special identity.

Another way to see the state is to pick a place that features your favorite activity. It could be boating on Lake Sakakawea, cross-country skiing in Icelandic State Park, or horseback riding in the Badlands.

Painted Canyon is one of the sights to be seen in the Badlands of Theodore Roosevelt National Memorial Park.

Two interstate highways and seven U.S. highways cross North Dakota. Several state and county roads lead to secluded areas. However, like other states with severe winters, North Dakota closes many of its facilities between Labor Day and Memorial Day. Exceptionally hot, dry summers, like that of 1988, can also cause the closing of parks or recreation areas if there is a fire hazard.

ROUGH RIDER COUNTRY: THE OLD WEST

Hugging the Montana border for about 210 miles (338 kilometers), this western slice of North Dakota used to be one of the nation's secret treasures. It is still a treasure, but with better roads, it is no longer a secret.

In 1947, Congress established the Theodore Roosevelt National Memorial Park in North Dakota. A memorial to one of the country's most dedicated conservationists, it is the only national park in the state. The famed old cattle town of Medora, entrance to the south unit of the park, is about two hours south of

Theodore Roosevelt National Memorial Park is home to a variety of animals, including mule deer (above). In the north unit of the park, petrified wood rests on erosion pedestals (right).

Williston. The brilliantly colored tablelands, buttes, and conelike hills are little changed since 1883, when Teddy Roosevelt first came to the area. Herds of buffalo share the park with elk, deer, coyotes, bobcats, badgers, beavers, and jackrabbits. The north unit, about an hour's drive south of Williston, is rugged Badlands country, with petrified forests and its own Grand Canyon along the Little Missouri River. Both units together total some 70,000 acres (28,328 hectares) of grassland and badlands. Visitors can drive through the scenic south unit and the more austere and isolated north unit. Painted Canyon Overlook on I-94 provides a magnificent view of the Badlands.

Medora is North Dakota's own "Brigadoon," a surprise town in the middle of nowhere that appears both real and make-believe. It is worth a summer day or more by itself. The young Marquis de Mores, who set out to revolutionize meat packing in the 1880s, named the town for his wife. The couple's twenty-six-room

Fort Union Trading Post National Historic Site, southwest of Williston

Château de Mores is now a museum that houses the original furnishings.

Although the railroad reached Williston later than other cities, it has been an important western trading center since the days of the Fort Union Trading Post. Located in a section of western North Dakota with an exceptionally large oil reserve, Williston became a boomtown in the 1950s and again in the 1970s during heavy oil exploration and drilling. When oil prices dropped in the 1980s, however, Williston's prosperity also declined somewhat.

Southwest of Williston, where the Yellowstone and Missouri rivers join, stands Fort Union Trading Post National Historic Site. This was the largest and most influential trading post on the upper Missouri River, owned at one time by John Jacob Astor's American Fur Company. When the railroad came west and hostilities increased between white settlers and Indians, Fort Union's prosperity ended. When the National Park Service took over Fort Union in 1968, it was all grassland with some stone foundations and artifacts. Pottery, china, glass buttons, beer bottles, and parts of trapping gear were unearthed on the site of Fort Union. Restoration of the post is almost completed. A rebuilt Bourgeois House shows the thriving business and comfortable lifestyle of traders—at least at this posh post. Famous guests dined there, including naturalist John James Audubon and artist-historian George Catlin.

Nearby Fort Buford, an important outpost during the Indian Wars in the late 1870s and early 1880s, was the site of Chief Sitting Bull's surrender in 1881. It is now a state historic site and museum with pioneer and cavalry artifacts.

MISSOURI RIVER CORRIDOR

Between 1804 and 1806, Meriwether Lewis and William Clark spent more time in North Dakota than in any other state. North Dakota has designated two scenic highways in honor of Lewis and Clark: ND 1804 and ND 1806. Modern explorers can follow a 300-mile (483-kilometer) route along the Missouri River from the South Dakota border to Montana. The route winds through cities, past farms, ranches, and coal plants, onto Indian reservations, past national and state historic sites, and through five state parks. Markers or displays tell about the Lewis and Clark trip at thirty locations along the North Dakota portion of the national Lewis and Clark trail.

Langeliers Bay Recreation Area, just above the North Dakota-South Dakota state line, marks the site of the expedition's first night in North Dakota. At Double Ditch State Historic Site, just north of Bismarck on ND 1804, deep rings and mounds—earth-lodge remains—still can be seen. When the expedition passed this

The Knife River Indian
Villages National
Historic Site includes
the location where
Meriwether Lewis and
William Clark hired
Sakakawea to help
guide the expedition.

place in 1804, a small band of Sioux Indians were living in the
ruins of a Mandan village hundreds of years old.

Bismarck is worth a day or more all by itself. The Heritage
Center on the capitol grounds includes the State Museum, the
State Archives, and a historical research library. The nineteen-
story white Indiana limestone capitol is a striking focal point, and
it is North Dakota's tallest building.

The original Fort Mandan, where the Lewis and Clark
Expedition wintered with the Indians, was erased by the shifting
Missouri River. But a re-creation of the old fort stands in a
wooded park on the river just west of Washburn. A few miles
away, where the Knife and Missouri rivers come together near
Stanton, is the Knife River Indian Villages National Historic Site.
This was where Lewis and Clark hired Sakakawea to help guide
the expedition. Between three thousand and five thousand
Hidatsas and Mandans lived on the site. Remains of the earth-
lodge homes, fortifications, and trails made by the primitive
travois used to haul goods are still visible.

International Peace Garden ▲

● Rugby

Sully's Hill National Game Preserve ▲ ● Devils Lake

The Peace Tower at the International Peace Garden in the Turtle Mountains north of Bottineau

PEACE GARDEN COUNTRY

The Canadian province of Manitoba donated 1,451 acres (587 hectares) of wilderness land, and the state of North Dakota donated 888 acres (359 hectares) of agricultural land for the International Peace Garden. Nestled in the picturesque Turtle Mountains, the garden lies astride a section of the longest unfortified national boundary in the world. The garden has given rise to another North Dakota nickname, the Peace Garden State, which has long appeared on state license plates.

The garden, the only one of its kind in the world, commemorates the years of peace between Canada and the United States. Government money from both countries along with donations from private organizations paid for the buildings, gardens, and services.

Visitors can follow a nature drive on the Canadian side and a cultural drive on the United States side. There are formal gardens, hiking trails, eating areas, an amphitheater, an athletic camp, a peace tower, a bell tower, and a peace chapel. The Bulova Company donated an 18-foot (5-meter) floral clock.

The International Music Camp within the Peace Garden complex is one of North America's leading summer schools for the fine arts. Despite the name "Music Camp," it offers courses in all the visual and performing arts to thousands of students each summer. The Music Camp also sponsors the annual Old Time Fiddlers' Contest and the International Festival of the Arts.

Rugby is less than an hour's drive south of the International Peace Garden. A Geographical Center Pioneer Village and Museum near U.S. 2 and state route 3 marks the center of the North American continent.

About 60 miles (96 kilometers) southeast of Rugby is North Dakota's largest natural lake. Devils Lake and the surrounding area are filled with historical sites and recreation facilities. According to Indian legend, victorious Sioux were drowned in the storm-tossed lake while returning from battle. The Indians called the body of water Bad Spirit Lake, which settlers ultimately changed to Devils Lake. The region was once an important meeting place for the nationwide Chautauqua movement.

Today, Devils Lake is a growing recreation area with a new state park system opened in the late 1980s. Devils Lake State Park system is the key recreational development of the long-standing, multifaceted Garrison Diversion Project. Included are Graham's Island State Park, Shelver's Grove State Recreation Area, Black Tiger Bay State Recreation Area, and the Narrows State Recreation Area. Graham's Island is named for Captain Duncan Graham, who was the first known white settler in the area.

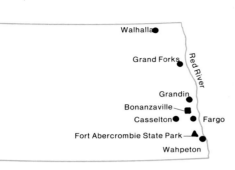

The Red River at Fargo

To the west of Devils Lake, Sully's Hill National Game Preserve offers a refuge for buffalo, elk, deer, and waterfowl. At the south end of Devils Lake stands Fort Totten Indian Reservation and the Fort Totten Historic Site. Many of the original buildings still stand, and it is one of the best-preserved forts from the era of Indian wars.

RED RIVER VALLEY

The Red River Valley is where it began for North Dakota. The first known white explorers traveled in this area and the first traders operated here. The first permanent settlement and the first universities were established here. The early railroads were built here and the early steamboats traveled on the Red River. Two-

Fargo, in the Red River Valley, is North Dakota's largest city.

wheeled Red River carts, developed by the métis in the area, negotiated the uneven prairie. The first bonanza farm was established near Casselton.

Fort Abercrombie, on the Red River just north of Wahpeton, was the first United States military fort in North Dakota. It was the terminus of several travel routes through the northern plains and the gateway to the Dakota frontier between 1857 and 1878.

The big cities as well as the farms are located in the Red River Valley. In between shopping sprees and seeing historical sites, visitors can tour such industrial plants as Steiger Tractor in Fargo and the North Dakota State Mill at Grand Forks.

Travelers to far-north Walhalla can tour the world's largest refinery that makes ethanol from barley, operated by Dawn Enterprises.

The map shows: Chase Lake National Wildlife Refuge, Arrowwood National Wildlife Refuge, Medina, Jamestown

The world's biggest buffalo is this huge statue that stands on a hill overlooking Jamestown.

North Dakota's oldest building is also at Walhalla. Norman Kittson, a key figure in developing trade between St. Paul, Minnesota, and the Pembina settlement, built the cabin in 1843-44.

Bonanzaville, USA, at West Fargo, is a restored pioneer village and museum with dozens of buildings, exhibits, and demonstrations.

THE PRAIRIE HEARTLAND

The Prairie Heartland, south of Peace Garden country and west of the Red River Valley region, is truly a nature-lover's paradise.

Thousands of prairie potholes, courtesy of the glaciers, dot the land. The Central Flyway passes over the Prairie Heartland, and huge flocks of waterfowl fill the sky during migration. At dawn and dusk, the prairie itself fills with ring-necked pheasants, sharp-tailed grouse, Hungarian partridges, and white-tailed deer.

There are five national wildlife refuges in the Prairie Heartland.

The Chase Lake National Wildlife Refuge, near Medina, is home to the largest white pelican breeding colony in North America. The Northern Prairie Wildlife Research Center, south of Jamestown on the James River, is one of only six major wildlife research facilities in the United States. Researchers at the center gather information that will help to properly manage and preserve certain species of wildlife in the Midwest, West, and Alaska.

Of the five national wildlife refuges in the Prairie Heartland, Arrowwood, north of Jamestown, offers the most for visitors. A list of some 250 species of birds found in the refuge and an auto tour brochure are available at the headquarters. Berry picking, boating, fishing, and limited fall hunting in certain areas also are allowed.

There is one site on the must-see list that is unlike any other in the Prairie Heartland. Standing sentinel on a hill overlooking Jamestown is the world's biggest buffalo—a 26-foot- (8-meter-) high statue of steel and concrete.

FACTS AT A GLANCE

GENERAL INFORMATION

Statehood: November 2, 1889, thirty-ninth state

Origin of Name: From the Dakota Indians who roamed the northern plains. Tribes joined together in friendship, and Dakota (or Dahkota) means "allies" in their language. The Dakota were also known as Sioux.

State Capital: Bismarck.

State Nickname: Flickertail State; also called the Peace Garden State, the Sioux State, and the Rough Rider State

State Flag: North Dakota's state flag, adopted March 3, 1911, is intended to be a copy of the regimental flag carried by the First North Dakota Infantry in the Spanish-American War and the Philippine Insurrection. An eagle with wings spread is centered on a field of blue silk. The eagle grasps a sheaf of arrows in one claw and an olive branch in the other. In its beak is a ribbon bearing the motto of the United States, *E Pluribus Unum*, meaning "from many, one." Above the eagle are thirteen stars topped by a golden sunburst. Below are the words "North Dakota." Across the eagle's chest is a red, white, and blue shield.

State Seal: The seal remains largely unchanged since the 1863 Seal of the Dakota Territory, though some modifications have been made through the years. The seal includes a tree in an open field, the trunk surrounded by bundles of wheat. A plow, an anvil, a sledge, a bow with three arrows, and an Indian on horseback pursuing a buffalo toward the setting sun signify the work and history of North Dakotans. A half-circle of forty-two stars stands for the number of states in the Union after North Dakota (and South Dakota, Montana, and Washington) were admitted in 1889. Around the circular seal are the words "The Great Seal/State of North Dakota/October 1, 1889." (On October 1, voters adopted their state constitution and considered that the date of statehood, though North Dakota was not officially admitted to the Union until November 2.)

State Motto: Liberty and Union, Now and Forever, One and Inseparable

State Bird: Western meadowlark

State Flower: Wild prairie rose

State Tree: American elm

State Fish: Northern pike

State Grass: Western wheatgrass

State Fossil: Teredo petrified wood

State Beverage: Milk

State March: "Spirit of the Land," by James D. Ployhar; became the official march on March 6, 1975.

State Song: "North Dakota Hymn," words by James W. Foley and music by Dr. S. C. Putnam, adopted as the official state song March 15, 1947:

> North Dakota, North Dakota
> With thy prairies wide and free,
> All thy sons and daughters love thee,
> Fairest state from sea to sea;
> North Dakota, North Dakota,
> Here we pledge ourselves to thee.
> North Dakota, North Dakota,
> Here we pledge ourselves to thee.
>
> Hear thy loyal children singing,
> Songs of happiness and praise,
> Far and long the echoes ringing
> Through the vastness of thy ways—
> North Dakota, North Dakota,
> We will serve thee all our days.
> North Dakota, North Dakota,
> We will serve thee all our days.
>
> Onward, onward, onward going,
> Light of courage in thine eyes,
> Sweet the winds above thee blowing,
> Green thy fields and fair thy skies.
> North Dakota, North Dakota,
> Brave the Soul that in thee lies.
> North Dakota, North Dakota,
> Brave the Soul that in thee lies.
>
> God of freedom, all victorious,
> Give us souls serene and strong,
> Strength to make the future glorious
> Keep the echo of our song;
> North Dakota, North Dakota,
> In our hearts forever long.
> North Dakota, North Dakota,
> In our hearts forever long.

POPULATION

Population: 652,717, forty-sixth among the states

Population Density: 9.2 people per sq. mi. (3.5 people per km²), forty-fifth among the states

Population Distribution: North Dakotans have moved from farms to towns in large numbers during the last thirty years. From 1960 to 1980, North Dakotans living in urban areas—cities and towns of 2,500 or more people—rose from 35.2 to 48.8 percent of the state population. During the 1980s, the urban population equaled the rural population for the first time. The population estimate made by the U.S. Census Bureau for 1986 showed North Dakota urbanites outnumbering rural dwellers by .4 percent. The only cities with more than 10,000 people are these:

Fargo	61,383
Bismarck	44,485
Grand Forks	43,765
Minot	32,843
Jamestown	16,280
Dickinson	15,924
Mandan	15,513
Williston	13,336
West Fargo	10,099

(Population figures according to 1980 census)

Population Growth: Population rose in the first half of the 1980s but then began to decline. The peak growing years for North Dakota were between 1880 and 1910; peak population was reached in 1930, before the depression and drought took their toll.

Year	Population
1870	2,405
1880	36,909
1890	190,983
1900	319,146
1910	577,056
1920	646,872
1930	680,845
1940	641,935
1950	619,636
1960	632,446
1970	617,761
1980	652,717

(1870 and 1880 figures show population for the part of the Dakota Territory that became North Dakota)

GEOGRAPHY

Borders: States bordering North Dakota are Minnesota on the east, South Dakota on the south, and Montana on the west. The Canadian provinces of Saskatchewan and Manitoba are North Dakota's northern neighbors.

Highest Point: White Butte, 3,506 ft. (1,069 m)

Lowest Point: Red River at Pembina, 750 ft. (229 m)

Greatest Distances: North to south—210 mi. (338 km)
East to west—360 mi. (579 km)

Area: 70,702 sq. mi. (183,118 km²)

Rank in Area Among the States: Seventeenth

Geographic Distinctions: The geographic center of the entire North American continent is located near Rugby.
Lake Sakakawea is the largest artificially made lake in the nation entirely within one state.

Rivers: North Dakota's major rivers and their tributaries total approximately 5,100 mi. (8,207 km). The two largest and most important rivers are the Missouri and the Red River of the North. The portion of the Red River between North Dakota and Minnesota forms a natural boundary. Both the Red and Missouri rivers provided transportation routes for people and goods in the early days of the territory and played vital roles in the development of Dakota. Both rivers have also destroyed parts of the state over the years with record floods.
The Missouri and the Red carry billions of gallons of runoff water annually. The two rivers and their tributaries provide a drainage system for most of North Dakota. The major tributaries of the Missouri River are the Knife, Heart, Cannonball, James, Little Missouri, and Yellowstone rivers. This river system drains approximately the western two-thirds of the state into the Gulf of Mexico. North Dakota tributaries of the Red River include the Sheyenne, Mouse, Pembina, Park, and Goose. Drainage from this system flows into Canada's Hudson Bay. Because the area east of the Sheyenne River drains north and the area west of the James River drains south, North Dakota claims a continental divide.

Lakes and Reservoirs: There are nearly 863,000 acres (349,247 hectares) of lakes and reservoirs in North Dakota. Although there are more than four hundred reservoirs in the state, Lake Sakakawea and Lake Oahe hold 97 percent of the total normal reservoir storage. Lake Sakakawea, with a surface area of some 368,000 acres (148,926 hectares), is the nation's largest artificially made lake within the boundaries of one state and one of the largest in the world. Lake Oahe is formed by South Dakota's Oahe Dam (on the Missouri River) and runs north into North Dakota. Hundreds of smaller lakes exist in the state, some natural and some created by dams. The state Water Conservation Commission maintains more than six

Moonrise from Wind Canyon in Theodore Roosevelt National Memorial Park

hundred dams. There are thousands of potholes and sloughs ("slews"), the natural reservoirs or small ponds created by glacier shift and melt-off. Some disappear during dry weather and fill with spring rains and melted snow.

Internal lake drainage systems receive some of the runoff not carried away by the rivers. Three of these are the Devils Lake, Long Lake, and Powers Lake systems, which include more than a dozen different lakes. Devils Lake itself is the largest natural lake in the state. Because it has no outlet except evaporation, minerals brought in by runoff have made Devils Lake brackish, or salty. Plans call for freshening Devils Lake through the Garrison Diversion Project.

Topography: North Dakota's predominantly flat surface actually has three distinct physiographic, or topographic, regions rising like steps across the state. From east to west are the long, narrow Red River Valley, the gently rolling Drift Prairie, and the more rugged Missouri Plateau. The Red River Valley, which has some of the richest soil in the world, is the bottom of glacial Lake Agassiz that once covered parts of North Dakota, Minnesota, and Canada. Its elevation is approximately 800 to 1,000 ft. (244 to 305 m) above sea level. The Pembina (or Manitoba) Escarpment, a sharp rise of 300 to 500 ft. (91 to 152 m), divides the Red River Valley from the Drift Prairie. An outstanding section of the Drift Prairie is the Turtle Mountains, a partially wooded rolling plateau that reaches 400 to 600 ft. (122 to 183 m) above the surrounding plains. The Drift Prairie is North Dakota's lake and prairie pothole region, a legacy of the long-gone glaciers. The Missouri Escarpment, hills that rise 300 to 400 ft. (91 to 122 m), separates the Drift Prairie from the Missouri Plateau. West of the Missouri River in this region is the Slope, an area formed not by glaciers but by wind and water erosion. The Badlands along the Little Missouri River are a spectacular example of the effect of erosion.

Climate: Because it is exactly in the middle of the North American continent, North Dakota has a continental climate: distinct changes of season, light to moderate rainfall, low relative humidity, and a lot of sunshine. The wind blows almost all the time, traveling rapidly across the plains without the interference

Wild morning glories (top right), prickly pear cactus (bottom right), and cottonwood trees (far right) are found throughout North Dakota.

from the forests or mountains found in other states. As a result, dust storms and blizzards are legendary.

North Dakota has endured more bad press due to weather extremes than any other state. Temperature variations from winter to summer are among the greatest on the entire continent. The record low of -60° F. (-51° C) at Parshall and the record high of 121° F. (49° C) at Steele occurred just five months apart in 1936. The average January temperature is 3° F. (-16° C) in the northeast and 14° F. (-10° C) in the southwest. The average July temperature is 67° F. (19° C) in the north and 73° F. (23° C) in the south. Average precipitation for the state is less than 17 in. (43 cm), with 20 to 22 in. (51 to 56 cm) of rain over the Red River Valley and only 14 to 15 in. (36 to 38 cm) of rain over the western Missouri Plateau. Average annual snowfall is 32 in. (81 cm). Although North Dakota has four distinct seasons, cold weather typical of winter can stretch over eight months.

NATURE

Trees: Found throughout the state are ashes, aspens, birches, box elders, basswoods, American elms, cottonwoods, willows, and bur oaks. Ponderosa pines and Rocky Mountain junipers grow in the Badlands. Shelterbelt trees planted to protect soil, game, and birds from the strong winds include Russian olives, Siberian (Chinese) elms, Black Hills white spruces, and Colorado blue spruces.

Wild Plants: Wild prairie roses, pasqueflowers, prairie phloxes, wild snapdragons, wild parsley, white meadow rue, meadow parsnips, harebells, native pentstemons, native lilies, prairie mallows, black-eyed Susans, columbine, star-of-Bethlehems, yellow star flowers, gentians, and wild morning glories can be found. Western prairie white-fringed orchids grow in the Sheyenne National Grasslands. Shrubs and vines include chokecherries, Juneberries, buffalo berries, high bush cranberries, wild plums, and wild grapes.

Animals: White-tailed deer, mule deer, moose, elk, pronghorn antelopes, bighorn sheep, buffalo (reintroduced in protected herds after near extinction), beavers, badgers, coyotes, minks, weasels, cottontails and jackrabbits, skunks, and ground squirrels can be found in various parts of the state. The Richardson ground squirrel, or Flickertail, gives the state its nickname. There are also frogs, toads, lizards, snakes (including the poisonous prairie rattlers), and snapping, Western painted, and soft-shelled turtles.

Birds: Nearly four hundred species of birds can be found in North Dakota. Among the most unusual are Baird's sparrows, LeConte's sparrows, Sprague's pipits, piping plovers, ferruginous hawks, least terns, upland sandpipers, chestnut-collared longspurs, bobolinks, and prairie chickens. Some of the approximately one hundred remaining whooping cranes (the tallest bird in North America) migrate through North Dakota each spring and fall. The largest breeding grounds in the world for the white pelican are at Chase Lake. Other game and songbirds include great blue herons, western grebes, pine warblers, woodpeckers, sharp-tailed grouse, ring-necked pheasants, Hungarian partridges, mourning doves, wild turkeys, owls, bald eagles, Western meadowlarks, orioles, and blue jays.

Fish: About sixty species of fish live in North Dakota waters, including walleyes, northern pike, saugers, perch, bass, catfish, bullheads, crappies, bluegills, sturgeons, coho salmon, and chinook salmon. Two federal fish hatcheries at Riverdale and Valley City stock some two hundred lakes and rivers.

GOVERNMENT

North Dakota's government, like the federal government, is divided into three branches: legislative, executive, and judicial. The Legislative Assembly, or state legislature, is made up of a 106-member house of representatives and a 53-member senate. Senators serve four-year terms; house members serve two-year terms. Half of the senators are elected every two years to preserve continuity. The legislators create new laws, rescind old ones, and amend the state constitution. They oversee the activities of government so that money is spent as intended and the powers given to state and local bodies are handled properly. Legislators approve key appointments made by the governor.

The executive branch, headed by the governor, administers the policy or law developed by the legislature. Governors are elected for four-year terms. There is no limit on the number of terms the governor may serve. The voters, however, can recall a governor from office in a special election. The governor prepares the state budget, calls special sessions of the legislature, grants reprieves and pardons to prisoners, signs or vetoes legislation, chairs numerous state boards and commissions, and appoints about twenty department heads who are directly accountable to the chief executive. The governor also heads the state militia.

The judicial branch interprets the law and tries cases. The five-member supreme court administers and supervises a "unified judicial system" consisting of district, county, and municipal courts. The unified system streamlines the judicial structure and assures equal standards for judges and courts in each county. In addition, the 1987 legislature provided for a temporary court of appeals to ease the overload of appeals cases before the supreme court. North Dakota's appellate court convened for the first time in October 1987. Supreme court justices are elected for staggered ten-year terms. District judges are elected for six years, county and municipal judges for terms of four years each. Judges on the appeals court are appointed by the chief justice of the state supreme court.

Number of Counties: 53

U.S. Representatives: 1

Electoral Votes: 3

Voting Qualifications: United States citizen, at least eighteen years of age, with thirty days residency in the precinct. (Voters who move within the state may vote in their old precinct until the thirty-day requirement is met in their new precinct.)

EDUCATION

The legislative assembly appropriates approximately 35 percent of state expenditures annually for education. The superintendent of public instruction is the chief executive of public elementary and secondary education in North Dakota. A state board of public school education has jurisdiction over school construction, reorganization of school districts, and tuition appeals.

North Dakota has 310 public school districts, 109 private schools, and 47 schools that are operated by the Bureau of Indian Affairs (BIA). The state also operates a State Industrial School at Mandan, the School for the Blind at Grand Forks, the School for the Deaf at Devils Lake, and Grafton State School for the mentally retarded. The Anne Carlson School at Jamestown is a private, nonprofit school for the multiply handicapped.

State colleges and universities are the University of North Dakota, at Grand Forks; North Dakota State University, at Fargo; Minot State University, in Minot; Dickinson State University, in Dickinson; Valley City State College, in Valley City; and Mayville State University, in Mayville. Private institutions are the University of Mary, in Bismarck; Jamestown College, in Jamestown; and Trinity Bible Institute, in Ellendale. Two-year colleges include North Dakota State University-Bottineau; University of North Dakota-Lake Region at Devils Lake; University of North Dakota-Williston; North Dakota State College of Science, in Wahpeton; and Bismarck State College, in Bismarck. Tribal community colleges are located at Fort Berthold, Turtle Mountain, Fort Totten, and Standing Rock Indian reservations.

ECONOMY AND INDUSTRY

Principal Products:
Agriculture: Wheat (especially durum and hard red spring wheat), barley, flaxseed, sunflowers, pinto beans, rye, honey, sugar beets, oats, dry edible beans, potatoes, alfalfa and range hay, beef and dairy cattle, hogs, sheep, turkeys, bees
Manufacturing: Farm equipment, jewel bearings, food products, bee equipment,

bricks, electronics, construction materials, food-processing facilities (including sunflower-seed-oil crushing plants, flour mills, sugar-beet refineries, fertilizer-processing plants, and potato-processing plants)

Natural Resources: Fertile soil, nutritious grazing grasses, oil, lignite coal, natural gas, clays, clinker or scoria, cement rock, granite, limestone, bentonitic clay from volcanic ash, salt, sandstone, quartzite

Business and Trade: North Dakota has traditionally exported raw products to other states and imported most of its manufactured goods. It is attempting to increase its manufacturing operations. There are nearly six hundred manufacturing firms or branch plants in North Dakota. Most manufacturing and many retail businesses are related to agriculture, mining, and oil production.

Tourism has become a major industry, earning the state $600 to $700 million a year. A new industry in eastern North Dakota important to tourism is gambling. It is carefully regulated and taxed by the state. Proceeds go to nonprofit institutions.

Fargo is a medical, farm-service, manufacturing, and wholesale and retail trade center; Grand Forks is an educational and retail center; and Bismarck is a government center with growing energy, medical, and retail services. A state economic development commission works to retain, expand, and start industrial operations. In hopes of increasing international trade, North Dakota opened a trade office in Japan.

Communication: North Dakota has ten daily newspapers, eighty-five weekly and semi-weekly papers, four Indian newspapers, and nearly one hundred periodicals. The *Bismarck Tribune* , begun in 1873, is the oldest continuously published newspaper in the state. Both the *Tribune* and the *Fargo Forum* have won Pulitzer Prizes. News services include Associated Press (AP) in Fargo and Bismarck, and United Press International (UPI) in Fargo. Television saturation is among the highest in the nation. Almost two dozen television stations and four dozen cable services reach every part of the state. There are about three dozen each AM and FM radio stations.

Transportation: Municipal airports served by scheduled commercial airlines are located at Fargo, Grand Forks, Bismarck, Minot, Jamestown, Devils Lake, and Williston. There are more than one hundred additional secondary commercial and municipal airports and more than four hundred privately owned "flying farmer and rancher" airstrips. Commuter airline runs include Bismarck-Williston and Devils Lake-Jamestown-Minneapolis (Minnesota). For a hundred years, railroads were critical to North Dakota's growth and prosperity. Considerable "railroad abandonment," or discontinuation of service, has occurred over hundreds of miles of track. The Burlington Northern and Soo Line still operate some 4,000 mi. (6,437 km) of track through the state. Amtrak, traveling the old Great Northern route from Fargo through Williston on its way to the Pacific Northwest, provides the only North Dakota passenger service.

North Dakota, the first state to complete its assigned interstate highway mileage, has 571 mi. (919 km) of interstate. There are almost 6,700 mi. (10,782 km) of state primary and secondary roads. Seven bus lines offer scheduled interstate city service, and fifteen bus lines offer charter service within the state and to points outside the state.

SOCIAL AND CULTURAL LIFE

Museums: The State Museum, along with the State Archives and Research Library, is housed in the Heritage Center on the capitol grounds in Bismarck. Among the collections is an outstanding selection of Indian artifacts. An official state art gallery is housed at the University of North Dakota, at Grand Forks. There are also 74 local and county historical museums and 104 local and county historical societies throughout the state.

E'Lan Art Gallery, in Bismarck, exhibits both folk art and fine art—paintings, pottery, drawings, and sculpture by regional and national artists. The nonprofit gallery is housed in the former home of the late James W. Foley, one-time poet laureate of North Dakota and the lyricist of the state song. Bonanzaville, USA, at West Fargo, includes a regional museum of the Red River and the northern plains. There is an Indian museum at New Town, owned and operated by the Three Affiliated Tribes—Mandan, Arikara, and Hidatsa. The Broste Rock Museum at Parshall has exotic rocks and minerals from all over the world.

Libraries: There are nearly one hundred community, town, county, and regional public libraries in North Dakota. The State Library Directory also lists college, medical and hospital, legislative, law, and other specialized libraries. Both Minot and Grand Forks air force bases have libraries.

In the late 1980s, North Dakota public libraries had nearly two million books, magazines, tapes, films, and other print and nonprint materials. The Fargo and Grand Forks public libraries have the largest print collections, each with more than 140,000 volumes. Bookmobiles, important in the largely rural state, circulate more than 500,000 print and nonprint materials annually. Fargo's bookmobile circulates almost 73,000 fiction, nonfiction, and juvenile volumes in one year.

Performing Arts: The North Dakota Council on the Arts and the National Endowment for the Arts have given community opera, symphony, and theater a major boost throughout the state. In the mid-1980s, about ninety organizations received funds to support dance, symphony, opera, choral, and theater programs in North Dakota. Traveling theater troupes and guest musicians perform at universities, colleges, theaters, and civic centers every year. Three annual events have become known nationwide. They are the Dakota Cowboy Poetry Gathering at Medora on Memorial Day weekend, patterned after the widely featured cowboy poets' gathering held each year at Elko, Nevada; the Medora Musical held nightly through the summer in a natural outdoor amphitheater; and the International Old-Time Fiddlers' Contest and Festival of the Arts concerts at the International Peace Garden. The Old-Time Fiddlers compete for cash prizes and trophies in North Dakota, Manitoba (Canada), and international competitions.

Sports and Recreation: There are no professional sports teams in North Dakota, but there is a full range of sporting events nonetheless. The annual Prairie Rose State Games, patterned after the Olympics, began in 1987 to promote amateur sports in the state. Among the July games are track-and-field events, swimming, road races, horseshoes, tennis, volleyball, basketball, and softball. Fans follow high school and college sports enthusiastically, especially basketball and football. High school basketball tournaments are covered by television and are of major interest throughout the state. Soccer is also popular with North Dakotans, and hockey is the number one sport in the eastern part of the state.

Outdoor recreation is virtually unlimited. According to the state department of parks and recreation, biking is the number one participation sport. The department has mapped four scenic cross-country bike tours. North Dakota rivers and lakes, especially Lake Sakakawea, offer boating, fishing, swimming, and water skiing. Dozens of parks, nature preserves, and wildlife refuges as well as four state forests (in this prairie state!) and three national grasslands are major recreation areas for hiking, snowmobiling, cross-country skiing, camping, horseback trail riding, bird watching, canoeing, fishing, and hunting. Of North Dakota's nineteen state parks and recreation areas, five were opened in 1988-89. The Devils Lake system, with a total of 1,265 acres (512 hectares) is the key recreational development of the Garrison Diversion Project. Among the other sites rich in both natural beauty and history are Fort Abraham Lincoln State Park, just south of Mandan; Turtle River State Park, west of Grand Forks; Icelandic State Park, just west of Cavalier; Lake Metigoshe State Park, northeast of Bottineau; Lewis and Clark State Park, southeast of Williston; Lake Sakakawea State Park, on the south shore of the mammoth lake just north of Pick City; Fort Stevenson State Park, south of Garrison; Fort Ransom State Park, north of Fort Ransom; and Beaver Lake State Park, southeast of Napoleon.

Golfers have more than one hundred courses from which to choose. North Dakotans celebrate their ethnic origins and state history by staging annual festivals.

Historic Sites and Landmarks:

Camp Hancock State Historic Site, on the original town site of Bismarck, preserves part of the military installation originally named Camp Greeley. The name was changed to Camp Hancock in 1873.

Château de Mores State Historic Site, near Medora in the Badlands, is a reminder of the brief but busy years spent by the Marquis de Mores in North Dakota. Overlooking the authentically restored Old West town of Medora is the twenty-six-room Château de Mores, home of the marquis and his wife Medora.

Fort Buford State Historic Site, southwest of Williston, includes the original stone powder magazine and officers' quarters. The important military post, built in 1866, was the site of the surrender of Chief Sitting Bull in 1881.

Fort Totten State Historic Site, near Devils Lake, is one of the best-preserved western frontier military posts. It was built of logs in 1867 and rebuilt in 1868 of locally made bricks. The original buildings house a theater and museum.

Fort Union Trading Post National Historic Site, southwest of Williston where the Missouri and Yellowstone rivers join, was built by the American Fur Company in 1829. This post was the headquarters for trading beaver and buffalo hides with the Assiniboines, Crows, and Blackfeet. About half of the original structures have been rebuilt or repaired.

119

Knife River Indian Villages National Historic Site, near Stanton, preserves the remains of several earth-lodge village sites once occupied by Hidatsa, Mandan, and Arikara tribes. A walking tour includes the site where Toussaint Charbonneau and his wife Sakakawea were living when Lewis and Clark hired them as guides.

Menoken Indian Village State Historic Site, near Bismarck, contains a prehistoric earth-lodge village thought by many historians to have been visited by La Vérendrye in 1738.

Pembina State Historic Site, in Pembina, commemorates several "firsts" in the state: the first church and school, the first customs office, the first permanent white settlement, and the first organized county. Museum exhibits interpret the history of the area.

Walhalla State Historic Site, in Walhalla, is the location of fur trader Norman Kittson's cabin. Built in 1843-44, it is North Dakota's oldest surviving building.

Writing Rock State Historic Site, northeast of Grenora, was discovered by General Alfred Sully in 1864. The two boulders containing Indian pictographs, or picture-writing, carved into the granite are thought to be prehistoric.

Other Interesting Places to Visit:

Annunciation Priory, in Bismarck, was designed by noted architect Marcel Breuer, who also designed the Whitney Museum of American Art and the Pan Am Building in New York.

Assumption Abbey, at Richardton, was completed in 1910. The Romanesque and Gothic styles of the buildings create an old-European feeling on the North Dakota prairie.

Bonanzaville, USA, near West Fargo, is a pioneer village and museum that recalls North Dakota's bonanza farm era. Historical exhibits are contained in forty original, restored, and re-created buildings.

Cathedral Area Historic District, in downtown Bismarck, includes nearly sixty historic buildings.

David Thompson Monument, near Velva, is a globelike granite memorial that honors the pioneer geographer and explorer who visited the area in 1797 and was the first to accurately map North Dakota.

Garrison Dam, at Riverdale, is one of the largest rolled-earth dams in the world.

Geographic Center of North America Pioneer Village and Museum, at Rugby, marks the center of the North American continent.

Gunlogson Arboretum Nature Preserve, west of Cavalier and adjacent to Icelandic State Park, is a 100-acre (40-hectare) preserve for rare plants and animals.

The floral clock in the International Peace Garden

International Peace Garden, north of Dunseith on the Canadian border, is a 2,300-acre (931-hectare) botanical garden that commemorates the long-standing friendship between the United States and Canada. Visitors may take self-guided scenic drives through the beautiful lakes, woods, formal gardens, and floral displays of the garden. Also on the grounds are hiking trails, picnic areas, an amphitheater, a peace chapel, and a large floral clock. The International Music Camp at nearby Bottineau is an outstanding fine-arts summer school.

North Dakota State Capitol, at Bismarck, is called the Skyscraper of the Plains. Designed in 1932, the nineteen-story building is still strikingly elegant and modern. The *North Dakota Heritage Center,* on the capitol grounds, houses the state historical society, the State Museum, and the State Archives. The *Governor's Residence,* the *Liberty Memorial Building,* an arboretum trail, and statues of *Sakakawea, A Pioneer Family,* and *Governor John Burke* are additional highlights of the capitol grounds.

Slant Indian Village, near Mandan at *Fort Abraham Lincoln State Park,* has reconstructed earth lodges on a site that was occupied by Mandan Indians from about 1650 to 1750.

Television Tower, near Blanchard, is the second-tallest structure in the world and the tallest in North America. The KTHI-TV tower, built in 1963, rises 2,063 feet (629 meters). The only structure taller than the KTHI tower is a radio mast in Poland, which is 2,120 feet (646 meters) high.

Theodore Roosevelt National Park occupies some 70,000 acres (28,328 hectares) of North Dakota Badlands and Prairie along the Little Missouri River. There are three units: the south unit, just north of Medora; the north unit, south of Watford City;

and Roosevelt's Elkhorn Ranch site, on the west bank of the Little Missouri River about half-way between the north and south units. Among the sights to be seen are buffalo, elk, native plants, and geological features such as petrified trees and colored clays. The nearby *Painted Canyon Scenic Overlook,* just east of Medora, provides one of the most spectacular views of the Badlands.

University of North Dakota, at Grand Forks, the state's oldest university, also houses the state art museum.

World's Largest Buffalo, on a hill overlooking Jamestown, is a 60-ton (54-metric-ton) steel and concrete bison that is 26 feet (8 meters) high. A *Frontier Village* on the site includes a pioneer schoolhouse, drugstore, jail, print shop, church, railway depot and caboose, barbershop, and post office.

IMPORTANT DATES

9500 B.C.? — Knife River flint, North Dakota's first export commodity, is mined in present-day Dunn and Mercer counties

700 B.C.? — Ceramic containers are first used in the North Dakota region for cooking and storing food

550-410 B.C.? — Early Woodland peoples live along the James River in southeastern North Dakota

100 B.C.? — Middle Woodland peoples begin building burial mounds in North Dakota, including complex ceremonial centers; bows and arrows are first used

A.D. 1200? — The Jamestown mounds site, which flourished for more than a thousand years, is abandoned

1600? — There is new movement by Indian tribes across North Dakota: the Cheyenne live in earth lodges in the Sheyenne River Valley, the Hidatsa move west from Devils Lake to the Missouri River, and the Sioux move from the Minnesota woodlands to the Dakota plains

1610 — Navigator and explorer Henry Hudson claims for England areas drained by Hudson Bay (the Hudson Bay watershed, which includes a large part of northern and eastern North Dakota)

1682 — French explorer René-Robert Cavelier, Sieur de La Salle, claims the entire Mississippi River drainage basin for his king, Louis XIV of France; the territory, called Louisiana, includes the Missouri River drainage basin in North Dakota

1738 — Pierre Gaultier de Varennes, Sieur de La Vérendrye, visits Mandan villages near the Missouri River and becomes the first European to leave a written record of his travels through North Dakota

1762—Land claimed by La Salle for France is ceded to Spain and a portion of North Dakota is now under the Spanish flag

1797—French trader Charles Chaboillez establishes a fur-trading post at Pembina, the first to be entirely within North Dakota; geographer David Thompson is the first person to map accurately a large portion of North Dakota

1801—Alexander Henry the Younger builds a fur-trading post at Pembina that becomes a nucleus for the first white settlement in North Dakota

1803—Spain returns the Missouri watershed to France; the United States, through the Louisiana Purchase, becomes the owner of this major section of North Dakota

1804-05—The Lewis and Clark Expedition, traveling from St. Louis to the Pacific Coast, winters in North Dakota; Lewis and Clark build Fort Mandan near present-day Washburn

1809—Manuel Lisa, a St. Louis trader and businessman who organized the Missouri Fur Company, leads the first American search for Missouri River trading fort sites

1812—In the first attempt at colonization by Europeans in North Dakota, Scottish nobleman Thomas Douglas, Earl of Selkirk, establishes the Selkirk colony

1818—Father Sévère Dumoulin opens the first church in North Dakota, a Roman Catholic mission at Pembina; the first North Dakota school opens in connection with the mission; another Catholic priest, Father Joseph Norbert Provencher, establishes a mission near that of Father Dumoulin in the Red River region

1829—Fort Union Trading Post is built on the upper Missouri

1842—Sturdy Red River ox carts begin a major commerce route between St. Joseph (now Walhalla) and St. Paul, Minnesota

1848—The first Protestant church service in North Dakota is conducted by Reverend Alonzo Barnard, a Presbyterian, and James Tanner, a Baptist

1857—The first military post, Fort Abercrombie, is established on the Red River

1861—The Dakota Territory is officially organized by the federal government, a step toward statehood, and President Abraham Lincoln appoints William Jayne the first territorial governor

1863—North Dakota is opened for homesteading under the federal Homestead Act of 1862

1867—Sisseton and Wahpeton Sioux cede lands to the federal government by treaty; the U.S. government establishes Fort Totten Indian Reservation

1868—Sioux chiefs and federal officials hold a major peace council at Fort Rice that results in the Laramie Treaty, which gives the Teton Sioux a 22,000,000-acre (8,903,180-hectare) reservation west of the Missouri River, part of which becomes the Standing Rock Reservation

1870s—A sale of government and railroad lands spurs the first North Dakota land boom; the population increases from 2,405 in 1870 to 36,909 in 1880

1870—The Fort Berthold Indian Reservation is established on the upper Missouri River; most of eastern North Dakota is ceded to the federal government through treaties with the Sioux and Chippewa Indians

1872—The first rail service in North Dakota begins when the Northern Pacific crosses the Red River from Moorhead, Minnesota, to Fargo

1873—The Northern Pacific brings the printing press for the *Bismarck Tribune* and the first edition of the paper, now the state's oldest, appears July 11

1875—Bonanza wheat farms, the mammoth agribusinesses of northern Dakota, begin in the Red River Valley; the United States government permits white settlement on Indian lands in violation of the Laramie Treaty, resulting in major Indian uprisings

1876—General George Armstrong Custer and the Seventh Cavalry leave from Fort Abraham Lincoln and are killed by the Sioux at the Little Big Horn River in Montana; the steamboat *Far West* sets a record by racing hundreds of miles in fifty-four hours, from the Little Big Horn River to Bismarck, with the news of General Custer's defeat

1882—The Turtle Mountain Indian Reservation is established

1883—The territorial capital is moved from Yankton, in southern Dakota, to Bismarck, in the northern part of the territory; a French nobleman, the Marquis de Mores, starts a meat packing plant and plans the town of Medora, named for his wife; Theodore Roosevelt visits Medora for the first time

1884—The University of North Dakota opens at Grand Forks with eleven students and four faculty members

1889—The Enabling Act provides for the division of Dakota into two states; delegates to the North Dakota Constitutional Convention draw up a state constitution, which is passed on October 1; President Benjamin Harrison admits North Dakota as the thirty-ninth state on November 2

1915—The Nonpartisan League (NPL) is organized to improve farm-business conditions in the state

1917—The Independent Voters' Association (IVA) is organized to oppose the programs of the NPL

1919 — The Bank of North Dakota is established at Bismarck

1920 — Voters add a recall measure to the state constitution, allowing the electorate to recall, or remove, state officials by special election

1921 — Governor Lynn J. Frazier is recalled by the voters, the only successful recall of a governor in the nation until 1988

1922 — North Dakota's first radio station, WDAY, broadcasts from Fargo; the State Mill and Elevator, born of efforts by the NPL, opens at Grand Forks

1930s — Drought, dust, and the depression plague North Dakota farmers throughout the 1930s; winds blow topsoil all the way to the Atlantic Ocean, creating dust bowl conditions; North Dakotans, unable to make a living in their state during the Great Depression, leave by the thousands

1930 — The most severe windstorms on record damage 1,847 buildings in the state; fire destroys the old state capitol

1932 — Fifty thousand people gather to dedicate the International Peace Garden in North Dakota and Manitoba, Canada

1944 — Congress approves the Pick-Sloan Plan to harness and develop the Missouri River; Garrison Dam is North Dakota's premier project under the plan

1947 — President Harry S. Truman signs a bill creating Theodore Roosevelt National Memorial Park

1951 — Oil is discovered on the Clarence Iverson farm near Tioga; voter registration is repealed, making North Dakota the only state without this requirement

1956 — The Nonpartisan League and the Democratic party merge; Garrison Dam power is generated

1961 — Fargo's Roger Maris breaks Babe Ruth's single-season home-run record

1965 — President Lyndon B. Johnson signs a law authorizing the Garrison Diversion Project to divert water from the Missouri River for farm irrigation, city water supplies, and recreational uses

1971 — The state constitutional convention is held in Bismarck

1972 — North Dakota's first rural water system, the Grand Forks-Traill Water Users' Association, begins operation; wheat prices almost double following huge grain sales to Red China and the Soviet Union; new state constitution is defeated by voters

1973 — The state's only Vietnam prisoner of war, Captain Loren Torkelson of Crosby, returns

1979—An oil boom begins in western North Dakota; spring floods make twenty-three of the state's fifty-three counties eligible for disaster assistance

1980—Construction begins near Beulah on the nation's first coal-gasification plant (to convert lignite to synthetic gas for power)

1988—The hottest, driest growing season in fifty years ruins crops and forces farmers to sell livestock; pre-Centennial celebrations begin

1989—The legislature passes a bill legalizing home schooling for children; November 2, marking one hundred years of statehood, climaxes the Centennial year

1990—The one-hundredth birthday of North Dakota State University of Agriculture and Applied Science at Fargo (originally North Dakota Agricultural College) and the one-hundredth birthday of the state's first two normal schools for training teachers (now Valley City State University and Mayville State University) are celebrated

ROBERT H. BAHMER

JOHN BURKE

IMPORTANT PEOPLE

Maxwell Anderson (1888-1959), lived and went to school in Jamestown; playwright; won the 1933 Pulitzer Prize in drama for *Both Your Houses*

Robert Henry Bahmer (1904-1990), born near Gardena; as head of the National Archives and Records Administration, he directed the presidential libraries of Herbert Hoover, Franklin Delano Roosevelt, Harry S. Truman, and Dwight David Eisenhower; received North Dakota's Rough Rider Award (1970)

Pierre Bottineau (1817-1895), a leading métis (of Chippewa and French heritage) in the Red River Valley during the mid-1880s; voyageur and trapper who led many expeditions across the northern plains

John Burke (1859-1937), son of Irish immigrants; came to North Dakota in 1888 as a young lawyer; practiced law in St. John, Rolla, and Devils Lake; served in the state legislature; governor (1907-12); treasurer of the United States (1913-21); justice of the North Dakota Supreme Court (1925-37); statue of Burke stands in nation's Capitol

George W. Cass (1810-1888), president of Northern Pacific Railroad; with Benjamin Cheney, a railroad director, purchased 13,440 acres (5,439 hectares) of railroad land near Casselton in 1874 to start the first bonanza farm

Charles Cavileer (1818-1902), customs collector and postmaster at Pembina in the early 1850s; helped to create the first permanent agricultural community in North Dakota by influencing settlers to come and farm

Charles Jean Baptiste Chaboillez (1736-1808), fur trader with the North West Company; in 1797 established briefly the first fur-trading post within North Dakota

Toussaint Charbonneau (1758?-1839), husband of Sakakawea; met Lewis and Clark at Fort Mandan; became their interpreter on the expedition

William Clark (1770-1838), explorer; co-leader with Meriwether Lewis of the 1804-06 Lewis and Clark Expedition to find a route to the Pacific Ocean; governor of Missouri Territory (1813-21)

Jay Cooke (1821-1905), financier; sold bonds worth $5 million to build Northern Pacific Railroad, opening North Dakota to vast new settlement; failure of Cooke's company led to the "Panic of '73," a nationwide depression during which railroad construction stopped

General George Armstrong Custer (1839-1876), army officer and Indian fighter; killed by Sioux Indians in the decisive Battle of the Little Big Horn in Montana, referred to as Custer's Last Stand; prior to battle was stationed at Fort Abraham Lincoln in North Dakota

Oliver Dalrymple (18??-1908), wheat farmer and lawyer; became manager and part owner of the Cass-Cheney Bonanza Farm, the first and most famous bonanza farm in the Red River Valley

Ronald N. Davies (1904-   ), lawyer, judge; Grand Forks lawyer (1930-55); U.S. district judge in Fargo (1955-   ); in 1957, he made a landmark ruling on racial integration in Little Rock, Arkansas while serving temporarily in that venue; received the Rough Rider Award (1987)

Angie Dickinson (1931-   ), born Angeline Brown in Kulm; actress and television star

Ivan Dmitri (1900-1968), grew up in North Dakota; photographer; born Levon West and well-known by that name for his etchings and watercolors; received Rough Rider Award (1962)

Thomas Douglas, fifth Earl of Selkirk (1771-1820), brought Irish and Scottish settlers to Manitoba, Canada, and northeastern North Dakota; founded the agricultural Selkirk Colony, or Red River Settlement

WILLIAM CLARK

JAY COOKE

RONALD N. DAVIES

ANGIE DICKINSON

CARL BEN EIELSON

LYNN FRAZIER

PHYLLIS FRELICH

BERTIN C. GAMBLE

Father Sévère J. N. Dumoulin (1793-1853), Roman Catholic missionary; with Father Joseph Provencher opened missions in the Red River Valley; in 1818, opened the first church in North Dakota, a Roman Catholic mission at Pembina

Carl Ben Eielson (1897-1929), born in Hatton; aviator; flew "on top of the world" from Alaska to the islands above Norway; helped to organize Alaskan Airways; was killed while trying to save passengers and cargo on a ship trapped in ice off North Cape Siberia; Eielson Air Force Base is located near Fairbanks, Alaska

Louise Erdrich (1954-   ), raised in Wahpeton; contemporary poet, novelist, and short-story writer; won a Nelson Algren Award for a short story; novels include *The Beet Queen, Love Medicine*, and *Tracks*

John Bernard Flannagan (1895-1942), born in Fargo; artist; widely exhibited, award-winning sculptor, known especially for his animal sculptures

James W. Foley (1874-1939), lived in Medora and Bismarck; poet; North Dakota poet laureate; he wrote the words to the state song, "North Dakota Hymn"

Lynn Frazier (1874-1947), homesteaded near Hoople; politician; governor (1917-21); recalled in 1921 (only the second governor in the nation recalled to date); U.S. senator (1922-40)

Phyllis Frelich (1944-   ), born at Devils Lake; actress; won a Tony Award for her role in the Broadway play *Children of a Lesser God* (1981); a founding member of the National Theater of the Deaf; received the Rough Rider Award (1981) and the Governor's Award for the Arts (1981)

Bertin C. Gamble, (1898-1986), raised in Hunter and Arthur; retailer; helped develop Gamble-Skogmo stores, one of the largest retail chains in the country; received the Rough Rider Award (1972)

Alexander Griggs (1838-1903), early Red River Valley settler; steamboat captain and flatboat operator on the Red River; founded, laid out, and helped to develop the city of Grand Forks; early Grand Forks mayor

Brynhild Haugland (1905-   ), born to Norwegian immigrant parents on a farm near Minot; state representative (1939-1990); honored by the North Dakota Legislative Assembly in 1989 as the senior legislator in the United States after fifty years in the state house of representatives

Alexander Henry the Younger (17??-1814), fur trader; established a trading post on the Red River at Pembina that became the center of the fur trade on the Red River; he wrote a detailed account of life and trade in the Red River Valley from 1800-08; is thought to have been the first person to raise potatoes in the Red River Valley; a nephew of fur trapper Alexander Henry, Sr.

James J. Hill (1838-1916), railroad builder and financier; nicknamed the "Empire Builder" for turning the bankrupt Great Northern into one of America's major railroads; northern Dakota, served by the railroad line, was known as "Hill's Country"

Virgil Hill (1964-   ), grew up in Grand Forks and Williston; boxer; won the World Boxing Association light-heavyweight title (1987)

VIRGIL HILL

Dr. William Jayne (1826-1916), physician, politician; family physician of President Abraham Lincoln; Lincoln appointed him the first governor of Dakota Territory (1861)

Norman Kittson (1814-1888), fur trader at Pembina; the first postmaster of North Dakota (1851)

Louis L'Amour (1908-1988), born in Jamestown; writer; prolific author of popular Westerns and one of the world's most widely read writers; received the Rough Rider Award (1972), the Congressional Gold Medal for a lifetime of literary achievement (1983), and the Presidential Medal of Freedom (1984)

LOUIS L'AMOUR

William L. Langer (1886-1959), born near Casselton; politician; controversial but powerful leader of state politics during the 1930s; reorganized and revitalized the Nonpartisan League; governor (1933-34); removed from office after being convicted of improperly collecting campaign funds (1934); his conviction was reversed; reelected governor (1937-38); U.S. senator (1941-59)

Peggy Lee (1920-   ), born Norma Deloris Egstrom in Jamestown; motion-picture actress and singer; her autobiography, *Miss Peggy Lee*, was published in 1989; received an early Rough Rider Award

PEGGY LEE

William Lemke (1878-1950), moved to North Dakota as a child; lived in the Grand Forks and Cando areas; politician; as a leader of the Nonpartisan League, he fought hard against bankers and others who controlled North Dakota farmers; as U.S. representative (1933-41, 1943-50), he supported laws that would help farmers; was North Dakota's only presidential candidate (1936)

Manuel Lisa (1772-1820), fur trader, was considered the most knowledgeable and important fur trader on the upper Missouri River; established several trading posts on the Missouri, including Fort Lisa, which served the Knife River villages in North Dakota; known for his fair treatment of the Indians with whom he traded

Roger Maris (1934-1985), raised in Fargo; professional baseball player; he broke Babe Ruth's single-season home-run record in 1961 while playing for the New York Yankees; played for the St. Louis Cardinals when they won National League pennants in 1967 and 1968; received the Rough Rider Award

ROGER MARIS

ALEXANDER McKENZIE

CLIFFORD "FIDO" PURPUR

JOSEPH ROLETTE, JR.

SAKAKAWEA

Marquis de Mores (1858-1896), French nobleman and visionary; he saw the Badlands as an almost limitless source of business opportunities; from his arrival in 1883, his business ventures included horse breeding, cattle ranching, meat packing, and stagecoach service; founded the town of Medora; in 1886, de Mores and his family returned to France

Maximilian, Prince of Wied (1782-1867), German scientist; his observations of American Indians were an important scientific contribution; visited Fort Union and the Knife River villages with German artist Karl Bodmer; wrote an account of his winter at the Knife River villages in his book *Travels in the Interior of North America in the Years 1832 to 1834*

Alexander McKenzie (1856-1922), political machine boss; controlled both business and politics in North Dakota from the 1880s until 1906, when many of his machine candidates were defeated; often used his influence to benefit the Northern Pacific Railroad; held only one elective office (sheriff of Burleigh County)

Aloisius J. Muench (1889-1962), born in Milwaukee; Roman Catholic priest; bishop of Fargo (1935-59); first bishop of a small U.S. diocese to become a cardinal (1959)

James B. Power (1833-1912), land agent for the Northern Pacific Railroad and father of bonanza farming; convinced railroad officials George Cass and Benjamin Cheney to start their mammoth farming operation to show the nation North Dakota's agricultural potential

Clifford "Fido" Purpur (1921-   ), born in Grand Forks; first North Dakota native to play in the National Hockey League; inducted into the Sports Hall of Fame and the U.S. Hockey Hall of Fame; received the Rough Rider Award (1980)

Joseph Rolette, Jr. (1820-1871), pioneer fur trader; he filed the first homestead claim in North Dakota, in 1868

Theodore Roosevelt (1858-1919), twenty-sixth president of the United States (1901-09); North Dakota's most famous rancher; briefly operated two ranches in the Badlands; an early conservationist who had a lasting effect on the western region he loved; Theodore Roosevelt National Memorial Park is dedicated in his honor

Sakakawea (circa 1788-1884), Shoshone Indian woman who was the guide on the Lewis and Clark Expedition; captured by Hidatsa Indians as a girl, she was brought to Dakota; it is said that her name (usually spelled Sacajawea or Sacagawea) means "Bird Woman" in the Hidatsa language; a statue of her with her son Baptiste on her back stands on the state capitol grounds

Fritz Scholder (1937-   ), lived in Wahpeton; artist; has been the subject of public broadcasting films; received the North Dakota Governor's Award for the Arts (1982)

Eric Sevareid (1912-   ), born in Velva; writer and broadcast journalist; a reporter and news analyst, Sevareid covered World War II battlefields for CBS; among his books are *Not So Wild a Dream* and *This is Eric Sevareid*

ERIC SEVAREID

Sitting Bull (1834?-1890), legendary Sioux warrior and tribal chief on the Dakota plains; nemesis of the U.S. military forces in the late 1880s when white settlers and Indians were vying for land on the plains

Vilhjálmur Stefánsson (1879-1962), grew up in Mountain; arctic explorer; advised the U.S. government on the defense of Alaska during World War II; advised Pan Am airline on polar air routes in the 1930s and early 1940s

Dorothy Stickney (1900-   ), born in Dickinson; actress; daughter of a frontier doctor; one of the great leading ladies of the theater; co-starred with husband Howard Lindsay in the long-running Broadway hit *Life with Father*; received one of first Rough Rider Awards (1961)

SITTING BULL

James Tanner (1800?-1864), Baptist minister; introduced Protestantism to North Dakota; brought the Reverend Alonzo Barnard to Pembina; the two are credited with conducting the first Protestant church service in the state (1848)

David Thompson (1770-1857), astronomer and geographer; employee of the Hudson's Bay Company and the North West Company; made the first map of North Dakota

DAVID THOMPSON

Edward K. Thompson (1907-   ), raised in St. Thomas; editor and publisher; began his journalism career as editor of the *Foster County Independent* at Carrington and night city editor of the *Fargo Forum* (1927); an editor of *Life* magazine (1937-68); original editor and publisher of *Smithsonian* magazine (1969-81), consultant (1981-83), publisher (1983-   ); received the Rough Rider Award

Era Bell Thompson (1906-1986), raised in Driscoll; journalist; one of the most prominent black women journalists in the nation; co-managing editor and international editor of *Ebony* magazine (1951-70); first woman to hold an executive editorial position with Johnson Publishing Company in Chicago; traveled through eighteen African countries to gather material for one of her books, *Africa, Land of My Fathers*; received the Rough Rider Award (1976)

EDWARD K. THOMPSON

Arthur C. Townley (1880-1959), homesteaded near Beach in early 1900s; political reformer; organizer for the Socialist party in North Dakota; a founder and president of the Nonpartisan League

131

ARTHUR C. TOWNLEY

LAWRENCE WELK

Dr. Merton Utgaard (1914-), born in Maddock; music educator and conductor; won first prize two years in World Music Contest (1966, 1970); founder of the International Music Camp near Bottineau; recipient of North Dakota Governor's Award for the Arts

Pierre Gaultier de Varennes, Sieur de La Vérendrye (1685-1749), fur trader and explorer; the first white person known to visit North Dakota; he attempted to find a water route to the Pacific Ocean but ended his journey near Bismarck

Lawrence Welk (1903-), born on a farm near Strasburg; musician and entertainer; rose from solo accordionist who played local farm dances to one of the world's most popular television entertainers; brought his "champagne music" to audiences for more than twenty years; the first recipient of the Rough Rider Award (1961)

Larry Woiwode (1941-), born in Carrington; writer; award-winning novelist, short-story writer, and poet who draws on the beauty and remoteness of North Dakota for parts of his reflective fiction and poetry; his works have appeared in several volumes of *Best American Short Stories* and the *New Yorker* magazine; his novels include *Beyond the Bedroom Wall: A Family Album*, which was nominated for a National Book Award, and *Born Brothers*

GOVERNORS

John Miller	1889-1891	William Langer	1933-1934
Andrew H. Burke	1891-1893	Ole H. Olson	1934-1935
Eli C. D. Shortridge	1893-1895	Thomas H. Moodie	1935
Roger Allin	1895-1897	Walter Welford	1935-1937
Frank A. Briggs	1897-1898	William Langer	1937-1939
Joseph M. Devine	1898-1899	John Moses	1939-1945
Frederick B. Fancher	1899-1901	Fred F. Aandahl	1945-1951
Frank White	1901-1905	C. Norman Brunsdale	1951-1957
Elmore Y. Sarles	1905-1907	John Davis	1957-1961
John Burke	1907-1913	William L. Guy	1961-1973
Louis B. Hanna	1913-1917	Arthur A. Link	1973-1981
Lynn J. Frazier	1917-1921	Allen I. Olson	1981-1984
Ragnvold A. Nestos	1921-1925	George A. Sinner	1985-
Arthur G. Sorlie	1925-1928		
Walter J. Maddock	1928-1929		
George F. Shafer	1929-1933		

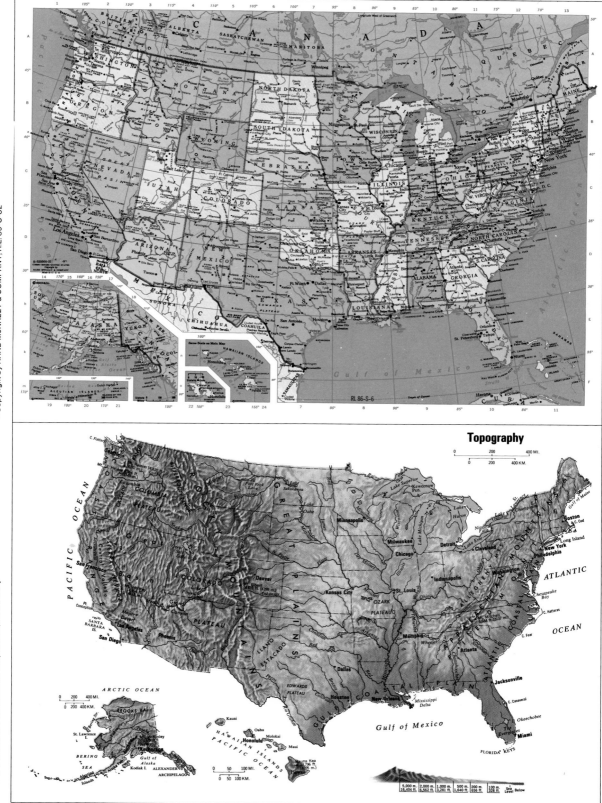

Topography

0   200   400 MI.

0   200   400 KM.

RL 86-S-6

5,000 m.   2,000 m.   1,000 m.   500 m.   200 m.   100 m.   Sea
16,404 ft. 6,562 ft. 3,281 ft. 1,640 ft. 656 ft. 328 ft. Level Below

MAP KEY

Place	Grid		Place	Grid
Abercrombie	C9		Chaffee	C9
Adams	A7		Christine	C9
Alamo	A2		Churchs Ferry	A7
Alexander	B2		Cleveland	C6
Alfred	C6		Cogswell	C8
Alkabo	A2		Coleharbor	B4
Alkaline Lake (lake)	C6		Colfax	C9
Almont	C4		Columbus	A3
Alsen	A7		Cooperstown	B7
Ambrose	A2		Courtenay	A7
Amenia	C9		Crary	A7
Amidon	C2		Crosby	A2
Anamoose	B5		Crystal	A8
Aneta	B8		Cut Bank Creek (creek)	A4
Antler	A4		Darling Lake (lake)	A5
Apple Valley	C5		Davenport	C8
Ardoch	A8		Dawson	C5
Argusville	C9		Dazey	B7
Arnegard	B2		De Lamere	C8
Arrowhead National Wildlife Refuge	C7		Deering	A4
Arrowwood Lake (lake)	B7		Denhoff	B5
Arthur	C8		Des Lacs	A4
Arvilla	B8		Des Lacs River (river)	A4
Ashley	C6		Devils Lake	A7
Badlands (wildlife preserve)	C2		Devils Lake (lake)	A6
Baldwin	C5		Dickey	C7
Balfour	B5		Dickinson	C3
Balta	B6		Dodge	C3
Barlow	C6		Donnybrook	A4
Battleview	A3		Douglas	B5
Beach	B1		Drayton	A8
Beaver Creek (creek)	A6		Driscoll	C5
Beaver Creek (creek)	B7		Dunn Center	C3
Belcourt	A6		Dunseith	A6
Belfield	C2		Dwight	C9
Berlin	C7		East Fairview	B1
Berthold	A4		Edgeley	C7
Beulah	C4		Edinburg	A8
Binford	B7		Edmore	A7
Bisbee	A6		Egeland	A6
Bismarck	C5		Eldridge	C6
Bottineau	A5		Elgin	C4
Bowbells	A3		Ellendale	C7
Bowdon	B6		Elm River (river)	B8
Bowesmont	A8		Emerado	B8
Bowman	C2		Enderlin	C8
Bowman-Haley Lake (reservoir)	C2		Epping	A3
Braddock	C5		Erie	B8
Bremen	B6		Esmond	B6
Brinsmade	A6		Fairdale	A7
Brocket	A7		Fairmount	C9
Buchanan	C6		Fargo	C8
Buffalo	C8		Fessenden	B6
Burlington	A4		Fingal	C8
Butte	B5		Finley	B8
Buxton	B8		Flasher	C4
Caledonia	B9		Flaxton	A3
Cando	A6		Forbes	C7
Cannon Ball	C5		Fordville	A8
Cannonball River (river)	C3		Forest River	A8
Carpio	A4		Forest River (river)	A8
Carrington	B6		Forman	C8
Carson	C4		Fort Berthold Indian Reservation	B3
Cartwright	B2		Fort Lincoln Estates	C5
Casselton	C8		Fort Ransom	C8
Cavalier	A8		Fort Totten	A6
Cayuga	C8		Fort Totten Indian Reservation	B6
Cedar Creek (creek)	C3			
Center	C4			

Place	Grid		Place	Grid
Fort Yates	C5		Granville	A5
Fortuna	A2		Great Bend	C9
Foxholm	A4		Grenora	A2
Fredonia	C6		Gwinner	C8
Fullerton	C7		Hague	C6
Gackle	C6		Halliday	C3
Galchutt	C9		Hamilton	A8
Galesburg	B8		Hampden	A7
Gardena	A5		Hankinson	C9
Gardner	B8		Hannaford	B7
Garrison	B4		Hannah	A7
Garrison Dam (dam)	B4		Harlow	B6
Gascoyne	C2		Harvey	B6
Geneseo	C8		Harwood	C9
Geographic Center of North America	A5		Hatton	B8
Gilby	A8		Havana	C8
Gladstone	C3		Hazelton	C5
Glen Ullin	C4		Hazen	C4
Glenburn	A4		Heart River (river)	C4
Glenfield	B7		Hebron	C4
Goldenvalley	C3		Heimdal	B6
Golva	C2		Hettinger	C2
Goodrich	B5		Hillsboro	B8
Goose River (river)	B8		Hoople	A8
Grace City	B7		Hope	C8
Grafton	A8		Horace	C8
Grand Forks	B8		Horsehead Lake (lake)	C5
Grand Forks Air Force Base	B8		Hunter	C8
Grandin	C8		Hurdsfield	B6
			Inkster	A8
			International Peace Gardens State Park	A5
			James River (river)	B6
			Jamestown	C7
			Jamestown Reservoir (reservoir)	B7
			Jim Lake (lake)	B7
			Joliette	A8
			Jud	C7
			Judson	C4
			Karlsruhe	A5
			Kathryn	C8
			Kenmare	A4
			Kensal	B7
			Killdeer	C3
			Killdeer Mountains (mountains)	B3
			Kindred	C8
			Kintyre	C6
			Knife River (river)	B3
			Kramer	A5
			Kulm	C7
			La Moure	C7
			Lake Ashtabula (lake)	B8
			Lake Metigoshe	A5
			Lake Sakakawea (lake)	B3
			Lakota	A7
			Langdon	A7
			Lankin	A8
			Lansford	A4
			Larimore	B8
			Lawton	A7
			Leeds	A6
			Lefor	C3
			Lehr	C6
			Leonard	C8
			Lidgerwood	C8
			Lignite	A3
			Linton	C5
			Lisbon	C8
			Litchville	C7
			Little Missouri River (river)	B7

Place	Grid		Place	Grid
Little Muddy River (river)	B2		Rolla	A6
Logan	C6		Roseglen	B4
Lonetree Reservoir (reservoir)	B5		Ross	A3
Long Lake (creek)	C5		Rugby	A6
Long Lake (lake)	C5		Ruso	C8
Maddock	B6		Ryder	B4
Makoti	B4		Sanborn	C7
Mandan	C5		Sarles	A6
Mandaree	B3		Sawyer	B4
Mantador	C8		Scranton	C2
Manvel	A8		Selfridge	C5
Maple River (river)	C8		Selz	B6
Maple River (river)	C8		Sentinel Butte	C2
Mapleton	C8		Sentinel Butte (butte)	C2
Marion	C7		Sharon	B8
Marmarth	C1		Sheldon	C8
Martin	B5		Sherwood	A4
Max	B4		Sheyenne	B6
Maxbass	A4		Sheyenne River (river)	C8
Mayville	B8		Solen	C5
McClusky	B5		Souris	A5
McClusky Canal (canal)	B5		Souris River (river)	A4
McGregor	A3		South Heart	C3
McHenry	B7		Spring Creek (creek)	B3
McKenzie	C5		St. Anthony	C5
McVille	B8		St. John	A6
Medina	C6		St. Thomas	A8
Medora	C2		Standing Rock Indian Reservation	C4
Mekinock	A8		Stanley	A3
Menoken	C5		Stanton	C4
Mercer	B5		Starkweather	A7
Michigan	A7		Steele	C6
Milnor	C8		Sterling	C5
Milton	A7		Stirum	C8
Minnewaukan	A6		Strasburg	C5
Minot	A4		Streeter	C6
Minot Air Force Base	A4		Stump Lake (lake)	A7
Missouri River (river)	C5		Surrey	A4
Minto	A8		Sutton	B6
Moffit	C5		Sykeston	B6
Mohall	A4		Tappen	C6
Montpelier	C7		Taylor	C3
Mooreton	C9		Theodore Roosevelt National Park	B2
Mott	C3		Thompson	B8
Mountain	A8		Tioga	A3
Munich	A7		Tokio	A6
Napoleon	C6		Tolley	A4
Nash	A8		Tolna	A7
Neche	A8		Tower City	C8
Nekoma	A7		Towner	A5
New England	C2		Trenton	B2
New Hradec	C3		Tschida Lake (lake)	C4
New Leipzig	C4		Turtle Lake	B5
New Rockford	B6		Turtle Mountain Indian Reservation	A6
New Salem	C4		Turtle Mountains (mountains)	A5
New Town	B3		Tuttle	B5
Newburg	A5		Underwood	B4
Niagara	B8		Upham	A5
Noonan	A2		Valley City	C8
Northwood	B8		Velva	B5
Nortonville	C7		Velva Canal (canal)	B5
Oakes	C7		Verona	C7
Oakwood	A8		Wahpeton	C9
Oberon	B7		Walcott	C8
Oriska	C8		Wales	A7
Osnabrock	A7		Walhalla	A8
Page	C8		Warsaw	A8
Palermo	A3		Warwick	B7
Park River	A8		Washburn	B4
Park River (river)	A8		Watford City	B2
Parshall	B3		Webster	A7
Pekin	B7		West Fargo	C9
Pembina	A8		Westfield	C5
Pembina Mountains (mountains)	A8		Westhope	A4
Pembina River (river)	A8		Wheatland	C8
Petersburg	B8		Wheelock	A2
Pettibone	C6		White Butte (butte)	C2
Pick City	B4		White Earth	A3
Pillsbury	B8		White Shield	B4
Pingree	C6		Whitman	A6
Pipestem Creek (creek)	B6		Wild Rice River (river)	C8
Pisek	A8		Wildrose	A2
Plaza	A4		Williston	A2
Portal	A3		Williston Basin (basin)	A1
Portland	B8		Willow City	A5
Powers Lake	A3		Wilton	B5
Raleigh	C4		Wimbledon	B7
Ray	A3		Wing	B5
Red River (river)	A8		Wishek	C6
Reeder	C2		Wolford	A6
Regent	C3		Woodworth	B6
Reynolds	B8		Wyndmere	C8
Rhame	C2		Yellowstone River (river)	B1
Richardton	C3		York	A6
Riverdale	B5		Ypsilanti	C7
Robinson	C6		Zahl	A2
Rocklake	A6		Zap	B4
Rolette	A6		Zeeland	D6

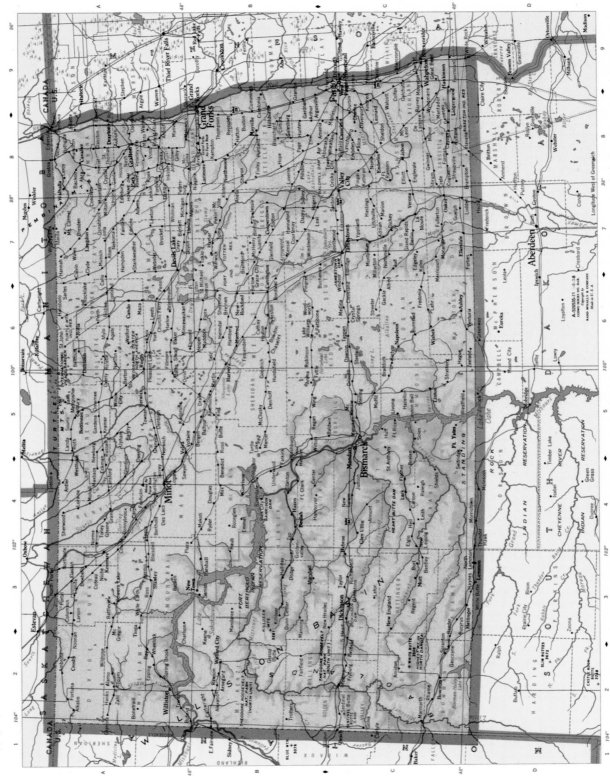

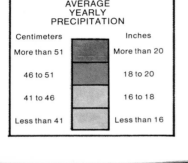

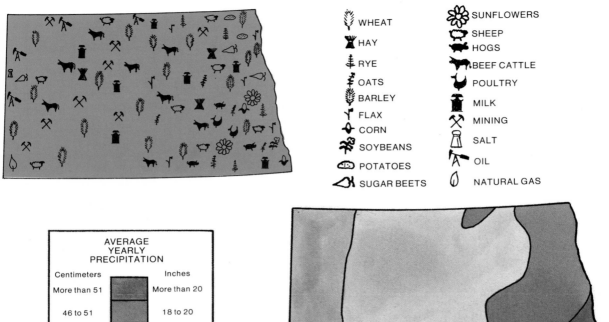

WHEAT	SUNFLOWERS
HAY	SHEEP
RYE	HOGS
OATS	BEEF CATTLE
BARLEY	POULTRY
FLAX	MILK
CORN	MINING
SOYBEANS	SALT
POTATOES	OIL
SUGAR BEETS	NATURAL GAS

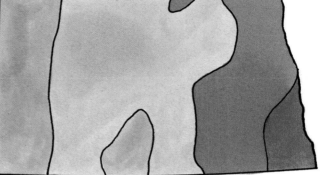

AVERAGE
YEARLY
PRECIPITATION

Centimeters		Inches
More than 51		More than 20
46 to 51		18 to 20
41 to 46		16 to 18
Less than 41		Less than 16

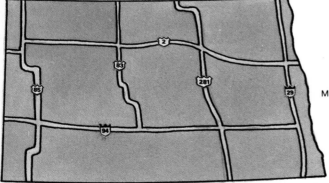

MAJOR HIGHWAYS

POPULATION
DENSITY

Number of persons per square kilometer		Number of persons per square mile
More than 10		More than 25
4 to 10		10 to 25
2 to 4		5 to 10
Less than 2		Less than 5

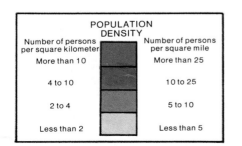

TOPOGRAPHY

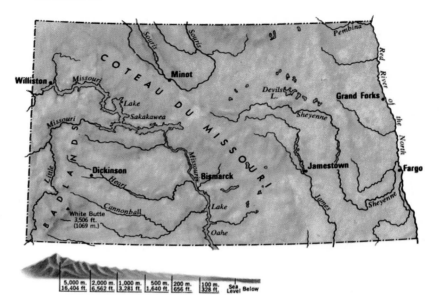

5,000 m. | 2,000 m. | 1,000 m. | 500 m. | 200 m. | 100 m. | Sea | Below
16,404 ft. | 6,562 ft. | 3,281 ft. | 1,640 ft. | 656 ft. | 328 ft. | Level |

Courtesy of Hammond, Incorporated
Maplewood, New Jersey

COUNTIES

Lake Sakakawea

INDEX

Page numbers that appear in boldface type indicate illustrations

A Pioneer Family, **one of the statues on the state capitol grounds**

Picture Identifications

Front cover: Wind Canyon, Little Missouri River, Theodore Roosevelt National Memorial
Park
Back cover: Contour planting in eastern North Dakota
Pages 2-3: Erosion in the Badlands, Theodore Roosevelt National Memorial Park
Page 6: One of North Dakota's Native Americans taking part in the state's Centennial
celebration
Pages 8-9: Bison in Theodore Roosevelt National Memorial Park
Page 22: A montage of North Dakotans
Pages 28-29: *Indians Hunting the Bison,* after Karl Bodmer
Pages 44-45: North Dakota settlers photographed near their sod houses
Page 62: A North Dakota wheat harvest
Page 72: The capitol building, Bismarck
Pages 86-87: Sailing on Lake Sakakawea
Pages 94-95: The International Peace Garden on the North Dakota-Canada border
Page 108: Montage showing the state flag, state tree (American elm), state flower (wild prairie
rose), and state fossil (Teredo petrified wood)

About the Author

Marge Herguth is a Chicago-area free-lance writer who has a special
interest in North Dakota. Her mother grew up on a North Dakota farm just
a stone's throw from the state line, near Fairview, Montana. Several rela-
tives were homesteaders in western North Dakota and eastern Montana
around 1900. Marge, husband Bob, who writes for the *Chicago Sun-Times*,
and their college-age children have crossed the North Dakota plains many
summers to visit cousins who still farm and ranch there. She has written
features and technical articles for newspapers and magazines. This is her
first book.

Picture Acknowledgments

Front cover: © **Sheldon Green;** 2-3: © Stan Osolinski/**M.L. Dembinsky, Jr., Photography Associates**; 4: © Diana L. Stratton/**Tom Stack & Associates**; 5: © **Sheldon Green**; 6: © **Sheldon Green**; 8-9: © Stephen Trimble/**Root Resources**; 12: © **Sheldon Green**; 14: © **Garry Redmann**; 15: © **Jeff Greenberg**; 17 (top): © **Ed Cooper**; 17 (bottom left): © **Kirkendall/Spring**; 17 (bottom right): © Greg Ryan-Sally Beyer/**Root Resources**; 18: © **Kirkendall/Spring**; 22 (top left, top right, middle left): © **Jeff Greenberg**; 22 (bottom left): © Russ Hanson/**Root Resources**; 22 (bottom right): © **Sheldon Green**; 25: © **Reinhard Brucker**; 26: © **Garry Redmann**; 27: © **Jeff Greenberg**; 28-29: **Joslyn Art Museum, Omaha, Nebraska**; 31 (left): © **National Museum of American Art, Gift of Mrs. Joseph Harrison, Jr.;** 31 (top right, bottom right): © **Reinhard Brucker**; 32: **State Historical Society, North Dakota Heritage Center, Bismarck**; 34 (left): © **National Museum of American Art, Gift of Mrs. Joseph Harrison, Jr.;** 34 (right): **Joslyn Art Museum, Omaha, Nebraska**; 37: **State Historical Society, North Dakota Heritage Center, Bismarck**; 38: © **Sheldon Green**; 39: © **Reinhard Brucker**; 41: **Historical Pictures Service, Chicago**; 42 (left): **Historical Pictures Service, Chicago**; 42 (right): **State Historical Society, North Dakota Heritage Center, Bismarck**; 43: **North Wind Picture Archives**; 44-45: **Harrison Collection, State Historical Society, North Dakota Heritage Center, Bismarck**; 47: **Historical Pictures Service, Chicago**; 49: **Harrison Collection, State Historical Society, North Dakota Heritage Center, Bismarck**; 50: **Historical Pictures Service, Chicago**; 52: **Brown Collection, State Historical Society, North Dakota Heritage Center, Bismarck**; 53: **Brown Collection, State Historical Society, North Dakota Heritage Center, Bismarck**; 55 (top): **Harrison Collection, State Historical Society, North Dakota Heritage Center, Bismarck**; 55 (bottom left): **A.C.J. Farrell, photographer, State Historical Society, North Dakota Heritage Center, Bismarck**; 55 (bottom right): **Historical Pictures Service, Chicago**; 57: **Ella Bagg Egnes Collection, State Historical Society, North Dakota Heritage Center, Bismarck**; 58 (left): **State Historical Society, North Dakota Heritage Center, Bismarck**; 58 (right): © **Sheldon Green**; 59: © Stephen Trimble/**Root Resources**; 61: **State Historical Society, North Dakota Heritage Center, Bismarck**; 62: © **Garry Redmann**; 64: **State Historical Society, North Dakota Heritage Center, Bismarck**; 66: **State Historical Society, North Dakota Heritage Center, Bismarck**; 67: **State Historical Society, North Dakota Heritage Center, Bismarck**; 68: **State Historical Society, North Dakota Heritage Center, Bismarck**; 70: © **Reinhard Brucker**; 72: © **Garry Redmann**; 76: © Stephen Trimble/**Root Resources**; 78: © **Jeff Greenberg**; 79 (left): © **Cameramann International, Ltd.**; 79 (right): © **Jeff Greenberg**; 80 (left): © Robert Pettit/**M.L. Dembinsky, Jr., Photography Associates**; 80 (right): © **Garry Redmann**; 81 (right): © J.C. Allen and Son/**Root Resources**; 82 (left): © **Chip and Rosa Maria Peterson**; 82 (right): © **Sheldon Green**; 84: © W. Tim Westerberg/**Root Resources**; 86-87: © **Sheldon Green**; 89 (left): © Vera Bradshaw/**Root Resources**; 89 (right): © **Sheldon Green**; 90 (both pictures): © **Sheldon Green**; 91: © **Sheldon Green**; 94-95: © Raymond G. Barnes/**TSW-Click/Chicago**; 97 (left): © **Sheldon Green**; 97 (map): **Len Meents**; 98 (left): © **Keith Kramer**; 98 (right): © Greg Ryan-Sally Beyer/**Root Resources**; 99: © **Sheldon Green**; 101 (left): © **Sheldon Green**; 101 (map): **Len Meents**; 102 (map): **Len Meents**; 102 (right): © Raymond G. Barnes/**TSW-Click/Chicago Ltd.**; 104 (map): **Len Meents**; 104 (right): © **Sheldon Green**; 105: © Russ Hanson/**Root Resources**; 106 (map): **Len Meents**; 106 (right): © **Kranzler/Kingsley Communications**; 107: © Greg L. Ryan-Sally A. Beyer/**Root Resources**; 108 (background): **Photri**; 108 (top): **Courtesy Flag Research Center, Winchester, Massachusetts 01890;** 108 (left): © **Jerry Hennen**; 108 (bottom): © **Reinhard Brucker**; 113: © Stephen Trimble/**Root Resources**; 114 (top left, bottom left): © **Virginia Grimes**; 114 (right): © **Keith Kramer**; 121: © Raymond G. Barnes/**TSW-Click/Chicago Ltd.**; 126 (top): **AP/Wide World Photos**; 126 (bottom): **State Historical Society, North Dakota Heritage Center, Bismarck**; 127 (Clark): **North Wind Picture Archives**; 127 (Cooke): **Historical Pictures Service, Chicago**; 127 (Davies and Dickinson): **AP/Wide World Photos**; 128 (Eielson, Frelich, and Gamble): **AP/Wide World Photos**; 128 (Frazier): **Historical Pictures Service, Chicago**; 129 (all four pictures): **AP/Wide World Photos**; 130 (McKenzie and Rolette): **State Historical Society, North Dakota Heritage Center, Bismarck**; 130 (Purpur): **AP/Wide World Photos**; 130 (Sakakawea): **Historical Pictures Service, Chicago**; 131 (Sevareid and Thompson): **AP/Wide World Photos**; 131 (Sitting Bull and Thompson): **Historical Pictures Service, Chicago**; 132 (top): **State Historical Society, North Dakota Heritage Center, Bismarck**; 132 (bottom): **AP/Wide World Photos**; 138: © **Jeff Greenberg**; 141: © James L. Ely/**Root Resources**; back cover: © Russ Hanson/**Root Resources**